Confessions of a Bad Mother

STEPHANIE CALMAN

Confessions of a Bad Mother

MACMILLAN

First published 2005 by Macmillan
an imprint of Pan Macmillan Ltd
Pan Macmillan, 20 New Wharf Road, London N1 9RR
Basingstoke and Oxford
Associated companies throughout the world
www.panmacmillan.com

ISBN 1 4050 5192 2

5 7 9 8 6 4

A CIP catalogue record for this book is available
from the British Library.

Typeset by SetSystems Ltd, Saffron Walden, Essex
Printed and bound in Great Britain by
Mackays of Chatham plc, Chatham, Kent

This book is rated 'PG'

Having children is a bit like assembling a shelf unit from a flatpack: you start off looking at the picture, sure you can do it perfectly. Then you get all the bits out and realize it's a bit more complicated than you thought. You start in with the screws and dowels, and quite soon you're overwhelmed. Getting tireder and more confused, you succumb to anxiety, anger and then panic. Finally, you shove it together, hide the bits you've left out, and just hope it doesn't collapse when there's anyone nearby.

This book is not a manual.

Contents

Contents

Contents

Acknowledgements

Mark Lucas, who steered me to George Morley, whose notes made me laugh.

You can't make a baby alone, even these days. And as the whole point of Bad Mothers Club is to ease the load, I would like to express my deep and lasting appreciation to those who did it for me:

Marie Thomas

Liz Irwin

Deborah Phillips

Anthony Silverstone

Dr Anne Szarewski

Dr Sarah Tunkel & Dr Penny Noble at the Fetal
    Medicine Centre

Tammy Whyte

Alison Salmon

Tilly Vosburgh

Acknowledgements

Claudia Stumpfl

Maggie Hamand

Angela Roche

Rose Prince

Nicholas Faith

Ruby Azhar

Katherine Shonfield

Joan Maker

Jessica Chappell

Joe Moran

Sally Graddock

Mary Banham

Pat O'Shea

Dr Edward Douek

Katarina

Wendy

Clare Tompkins

Nicky Oldfield

University College Hospital Neo-Natal Unit

Margaret Pyke Centre

Lucy Lindsay

Betsy Tobin

Amanda Brown

Judith Apter

Vida Adamoli

Sarah Litvinoff

Acknowledgements

For www.badmothersclub.com:

Sam Blagg

Anne O'Donovan, the original 'BM'

Jay Murphy, who helped show the way

Jay Nagley

Toni Morden

Becky Hill

Tony Slack

Kathryn Lamb

Jo Hage

Julia Porter

My mother, Pat McNeill, who said: 'Actually, I think
    you're doing really well.'

My sister, Claire Calman, who said – on more than one
    occasion: 'Would you like me to come round . . .?'

And . . .

My husband, Peter Grimsdale, who said: 'It'll be fine.'
    And – it hurts me to say this – he was right.

Prologue

We're in a pub in the West Country and Lydia has no chips. Lawrence's scampi has arrived with plenty, her fishcake with none. I know he can't possibly finish that huge pile, and I hate waste.

'Lawrence, can you give Lydia some of your chips?'

'No! Why should I?'

'Because she hasn't got any, and you've got loads.'

'It's not fair!'

Peter and I start to turn into badly dramatized versions of my parents.

'Why don't we just get some more chips?' (my father).

'Because he's got loads already, and is going to fill up on those and not eat his scampi as it is!' (my mother)

Being a female, I am engaged in the pointless process of distinguishing one fat-soaked component of the meal from another, to create a fictional nutritional hierarchy. Even as the meal degenerates into chaos, I notice that when it comes to the differences between the sexes, this is one of the most intriguing. Women use even the most rudimentary knowledge of food chemistry to at least attempt to care for their families by regulating their diets, whereas men tend to throw themselves down whichever route leads – they think – to an easy life. But the tactic that lends peace to the dinner table *now*, is often the cause of trouble *later* – of the *'Daddy always lets us have chips'* variety – frequently when Daddy is not around. This is called writing cheques your wife has to cash, and is one of the reasons women often want to hit their husbands with pans.

'Well, none of us can come up to your exacting standards,' says Peter, leaving the relatively constricting field of my parenting deficiencies for the wide-open prairie of my failed personality in general.

I ask my daughter: 'Lydia, would you like some of my potato instead?'

'No!'

'Lawrence, give Lydia some of your chips.'

'NO!!'

'*Right . . .*' I say this decisively, but fail to back it up with any kind of action, or even the rest of the sentence. Peter is now refusing to be either of my parents, and has cast himself as The Reasonable One.

'Can't we just have our meal?' he moans desperately, the innocent Red Cross worker caught between warring rebel factions.

This makes me want to punch him really hard.

'If you won't give Lydia any of your chips, you're not having any pudding.'

'Da-ddy . . .!'

'This is ridiculous.'

I take five of Lawrence's chips and put them on Lydia's plate.

'Thank you, Mummy,' says Lydia in her lion-cub voice.

'She took my chips!'

'Well done,' says Peter. 'Happy now?'

'I'll tell you what'd be great. If you'd just *once* back me up.'

'I'll never be able to do what you want, that's pretty clear.'

'You shit . . .'

'Mummy said shit!'

'Daddy! Mummy said s-h-one-t!'

'Brilliant!' says Peter. 'Well done.'

I want to hit him, and get out of this awful place with its purple carpet and pathetic attempt to be a brasserie by putting a copy of the *Mail on Sunday* on the bar. I want to scream at him, push him through the window and go back to the junction where I left my life, the manageable one. And even if it wasn't always manageable, it didn't keep suddenly getting away from me like this. I should never have become a parent. It's impossible. In the magazines, parenting looks like a cruise. When you get there, it's a tiny rowing boat, in a storm. And some bastard's not put in any oars.

1 Mother's Block

I wasn't going to have children. I was too frightened to have them, and I was sure I was physically and emotionally incapable of looking after them. Following the terrifying assault of birth, it would be one long, ever-repeating loop between the A&E department and the washing machine. And anyway, I wasn't the Maternal Type.

Whatever I was, it didn't appear to *be* a Type. I loved cartoons and comic strips, children's books and toys. I still had my Sindy, and her BOAC flight bag, on the shelf beside my desk. And I was intensely nostalgic about childhood games, especially 'Orphanages', when my sister and I placed our dolls in far corners of the flat, often with an arm or leg sticking out to indicate injury, then went round rescuing them with our pram. We often turned the bedroom into a dormitory, and by the age of about ten I was fantasizing in vivid detail about finding an abandoned baby in a phone box, which I would bring up to universal acclaim.

I loved the *idea* of fostering, adoption and rescue; it was just actual babies I didn't like. As a child I hated them coming round to play, resented the attention they got from my mother, and was infuriated by the implicit order of precedence that meant they were allowed to mess up my toys. As I got older, with the need for ready cash, I'd take any job so long as it didn't involve children. In my entire adolescence I babysat once, and that ended with the children playing football in the kitchen and my calling the seven year old a racist. (Well, he was.)

Yet, as I grew up, I failed to acquire the necessary credentials to qualify as a proper child-hater. I lived in a swamp of magazines, books and clothes. My home contained no porcelain lampstands, white carpets or thin, wobbly vases perched on stands. My surfaces weren't concrete or glass or slate. I failed art O level with the lowest grade possible and didn't even *want* to do architecture, interior design or any of the professions traditionally associated with extreme neatness. Anally, I just wasn't retentive enough.

I *wanted* to want children; I didn't enjoy feeling abnormal. I longed to join in, to see what all the fuss was about. I wanted to 'get it'. I had nurturing impulses, but they were all towards adults. I'd go to a meeting with a magazine editor, and end up addressing her relationship issues. I could stand at a bus stop while old people had a good moan to me about the Poll Tax, the dangers of loose paving stones or the rising cost of tinned salmon. Some people did aerobics for a hobby, or collected models of old buses. I had listening. I felt all warm and open, letting the shoals of problems wash over me. But uterine stirrings there were none. Maybe I just wasn't ready. One of these days I was bound to become the Maternal Type. I just had to be patient.

Nothing happened. I had relationships, as you do. I got involved with a very decent man who wanted us to marry and have a child. But we weren't right together. Meanwhile, without meaning to, I started drifting towards the children's departments of shops. In Marks & Spencer, I would slow down on the way to the food or cosmetics, and linger by the tiny, little socks. Then, when I thought no one was looking, I'd hold them, still on the rails, and cry.

I knew I was trespassing. I must have looked like those men in the lingerie department who don't quite seem to be shopping for their wives. After all, these were not the actions of an infertile woman, prevented from receiving the Greatest Gift of All by a curse of nature; the only thing stopping me from getting pregnant, was – as far as I knew – myself.

Then at twenty-seven I was diagnosed with polycystic ovaries, a well-known cause of infertility and in my case, something conveniently medical to hide behind. At least now I needn't mention my abnormal lack of maternal instinct. I could plead Biology. But the chances of any man in my life wanting to have children – if I did meet one I could stick with – were likely to increase with age. And even if *he* didn't want to, I would be supposed to start pressing for it. Any year now, wasn't panic supposed to set in? I would stand out even more as a freak.

One by one, my friends crossed the Great Divide. My friends' babies didn't mind me, and were even rather cute. But they didn't make me gasp inwardly, as I had at the Ferrari Museum: *'Dear God, Please, please, PLEASE let me have that 1964 Dino 246, I'll never ask for anything ever again, EVER!!'* And I didn't have to be removed from a baby by security guards for holding on too long and stroking its beautiful bonnet.

I passed my thirtieth birthday and saw Youth rolling away from me, as if down a hill. My father died. By now, I was surely supposed to feel *something*. As my friends' babies got bigger and began to move around the room unaided, it got worse. I knew I should be asking questions, but what? Was it about their food? Their pooh? When was the right moment to ask, *'And is he walking yet?'* But if you were sitting there in the same room as them, having coffee, it was bloody obvious! *'Does he – er, enjoy crawling?'* Was that it? It was worse than being abroad. When I went to China, I spoke no Mandarin, but had *something* in common with the giggling girls who approached me in the street; a mutual desire to connect. But on my home planet, I was an alien. Out with my friends for the evening, away from the visual cues, I kept off the subject, knowing I'd get it wrong.

Birth stories, oddly enough, I could listen to. They were a bit like really bad holidays, hilarious in their awfulness after the event, or car accidents; being squeamish has never stopped me from slowing down to look.

But I didn't want to give up my career – or what passed for one. I pottered along, writing articles and not making much money. It may not have been much of a career, but it was mine. My parents had friends who had become mothers and also worked, mainly by not doing the housework for thirty years. *That* I could sign up to. But I had trouble enough getting down to work as it was, and was sure children would ruin what little focus I had. And when I visited homes with small children, the constant interruptions meant a ten-minute anecdote could take an hour, because every five minutes a two year old would force the conversation to a halt. *'Mummeee!'* And not even for anything important! *'I want a biscuit!'* What, *now*? Couldn't they *wait*? Then I'd reboot myself, and it would happen again. And again. And again. I was at a loss to comprehend the inability of small children to be self-sufficient for more than thirty seconds at a time. Couldn't they just *go away*? And the mothers not only tolerated these outrages, but seemed not to mind! How could they let themselves be annexed by these tiny invaders, without even putting up a fight? Did they lose the will to be separate, to exist in their own right? It was as if they no longer had an outline, just a blur where their boundaries used to be.

And evenings weren't even sacred. I went to dinner at Rob and Cecily's. They both worked long hours and would, you'd think, have enjoyed some time together at the end of the day. There was another couple there I knew, Alex and Tim. I never thought it was possible to feel so much solidarity with gay men. We all sat with frozen smiles as six-year-old Hannah ran round and round, bashing the furniture and shouting. Rob and Cecily kept throwing each other nervous glances, as if waiting for the real parents to come in. Or did they believe some mysterious form of anti-gravity would magically waft her upstairs? Eight o'clock passed, and nine. 'Invited' to go to bed, she returned with all her bedding, which she dumped on the floor. By ten she was literally hurling herself against the walls. When she was finally carted off, Rob said: 'If you think that's bad, you should see her brother.'

I made a mental note to come back in ten years, the great benefit of teenagers being that they never want to be with the grown-ups.

Then I met Peter, and we were compatible in one major respect: our fear of being impulsive. We had lunch, then two years later, dinner. It was about the right pace – if you couldn't hear your biological clock.

But I still couldn't come down firmly against mother-hood. I had a double fear: fear of having children and fear of *not* having them. What if I got to fifty and felt bereft? That might be even worse! Maybe it was like skiing: if so many people were that keen, there must be something in it.

I decided to do some research. I was used to becoming an instant expert on subjects I had no previous knowledge of, so I'd just take the same approach. Researching was like revising for an exam; you spewed all the information into the article and for a very short period became an expert. My sister Claire, who worked for *Best* magazine, could remember everything she'd ever edited or written about: wine, Norway, mohair ... You could dial her up and say: *'What's that chemical in chocolate that makes you feel lovely?'* And she'd answer straight away: *'Phenylethylamine.'*

Could this work with motherhood? Did people investigate all the cots, drinking cups and bouncy walkers and by the time they gave birth, be somehow – qualified? If I began the research, would it lessen my anxiety and confusion? I didn't know, but there were two clear advantages. If I *did* decide to have kids, I'd at least know more than I knew now. And if I didn't, I'd have made my decision on an informed basis. Either way, it would give me the illusion of control, which always helps. When dealing with an issue completely driven by hormones and emotions, what better strategy than to try and blind yourself with science? I would follow the advice I'd got on a screenwriting course: when plagued by writer's block, go out and do research. There was no reason why it shouldn't work for mother's block as well.

But all that was, of course, only a way of avoiding looking at the really scary part. Although the actual birth counts for a very brief part of one's life, there was the most enormous emphasis on it – and not just from me. People gathered eagerly to tell me stories of pre-eclampsia, epidurals that worked only on one side, or too late, or not at all, thirty-six-hour labours that ended in emergency Caesareans, and postnatal incontinence. A friend of a friend was stitched up so badly that her sex life was finished. Another tore nearly all the way round so she thought she was going to rip in half. *'I knew it wasn't going*

well,' she said, 'when the consultant called, *"Hey everybody –
come and look at THIS!"'* And there were triumphant
natural ones, marvellous events in baths that were all
over in time for *Newsnight*. But I knew there was no way
of my achieving that. As someone who cried at a smear
test, I knew it was an impossibility. And anyway, there
was the loss of dignity. I just couldn't see what was
beautiful and moving about expelling a live creature –
covered in blood and slime – from the most private part
of you. And in front of other people! Were they really
asking me to believe that *I* could withstand an entirely
new person springing out of my body? I mean, I'd seen
something similar in *Alien*, and it looked like a hell of a
way to spend a Friday night. So what if I knew all these
people who'd done it? I knew someone who'd gone down
the Amazon with hallucinating, axe-wielding Yanomami
Indians and I didn't want to do that either.

In any case, whatever the method of delivery, I had
a problem with the very *concept* of conception itself. To
me this too lacked credibility. To start with, two cells
being the start of a wholly unique individual was frankly
stretching it. *Two cells*. Asexual reproduction made far
more sense. Take the hydra, from third year biology. A
dull green plant that didn't get out much, it would get so
far in life, then grow a baby hydra on the side of its body.
The baby then detached itself and went off to live an

independent life as a totally separate, dull green plant. That I could relate to. It didn't need weaning or nurturing, or any of that. It didn't have to split the mummy hydra half open to get out, and there was nothing in the book about the mummy hydra missing its freedom and getting depressed.

Still, I carried on gathering intelligence, even if it was almost entirely useless. I felt like an impostor, trying to choose a religion when I didn't even believe in God. But it was something to do. It felt objective and practical. If I woke up one morning feeling maternal, I'd have all the information at my fingertips. Or wherever. Maybe it was like becoming a priest; the Call could come at any time.

Sometimes, when you can't decide about something, Life decides for you. While visiting friends in Australia, Peter and I were in a car accident. When we came back, I was too feeble to manage on my own so the decision to move in together was made for us. We both mitigated our fear of commitment by pretending it was temporary.

'Just until I get stronger.'

'Of course, of course.'

'I won't bring too much stuff.'

'No, no.'

'Just my computer.'

'You've got to work.'

'And a few clothes and books. And maybe my mixer.'

'Mixer?'

'In case I feel like doing any baking.'

The domestic suffocation I'd been avoiding turned out to be a mirage. My God, I thought, as we lay on the sofa eating chocolate and watching *Thunderbirds*: I've been running away from *this*? My logic, that if I didn't live with someone they couldn't leave me, was possibly a teensy bit flawed. On that basis, you'd never eat a nice meal or watch a sunset or go to a film because at some point it had to end. *Life has to end, you jerk! Don't you think you've wasted enough of it already?*

Then we went to see some friends who'd just had a baby. They lived in a teeny-weeny house opposite a glue fac-tory; you bumped your head on everything, and there was this *smell*. While they were opening the wine, the moment came when they said – as people do – 'Would you like to hold him?'

And I thought: *No*, because when I hold babies they always cry. But Peter stepped forward and took him with great confidence, and smiled at him and put him upright against his shoulder, and he stopped crying and went all relaxed and sweet.

'Aren't you lovely?' he said to it. I didn't say anything. I thought of saying, *'How do you know what to do?'* or, *'If you could be the woman and I could be the man, we might be able to sort something out,'* but instead I just stood there trying to look normal.

I liked the way he looked holding the baby, but when I tried to imagine us with another person – someone who didn't exist yet – it was beyond me.

I mean, how was it decided what sort of child you would have? DNA, yes yes, but I only had to look at my own parents to see that could go wrong. If DNA was logical, I'd be tall, poetic and intellectual like my mother, instead of short, hairy-legged and moody like my dad. What if we had a child and didn't – relate to it? I'd read about normal, average couples who mysteriously produced maths geniuses. What if we had a lawyer? Or imagine a child who *liked football* – all mud, crowds and shouting – or worse, *cricket*? Quieter crowds and less mud, perhaps, but totally incomprehensible. We couldn't spend fifteen years in the pavilion.

The only children I had to go on were the ones I'd already met, and they hadn't so far engendered waves of maternal joy so much as the desire to be somewhere tidier and quieter. I had no sense of giving rise to a fresh being, a unique individual. I didn't see them as anything to do with *me* – or their perfectly normal father-in-waiting. I sort of imagined you picked them out from what was already there, like those sofa shops where they have a set choice of fabrics and styles: '*I suppose I'll have the loud, snotty one in the pink and white.*'

I had no wish to pick them up, or wipe their noses or, God forbid, look after them for any length of time. If their parents left the room for two seconds, I panicked. The command I most dreaded after, '*Pop your things off and open your knees,*' was, '*I can hear the baby crying; can you just finish giving x his lunch?*'

So when I tried to imagine my own, I was sure I'd feel the same way. What could possibly motivate me to pick up a spoon and go near any of that *stuff*? The stickiness, the sliminess of it, made me want to gag. Anyhow, as I wouldn't know how to get on with the actual child in the first place, I was doomed. I should just give up and Get on with My Life.

Then, one night, Peter took me to meet an Italian couple he knew. Their house was festooned with ornaments, pictures in curly, gold frames and tiny tables with just one thing on them. Very unchild-friendly.

We were introduced to Ilaria, their two-year-old daughter, and as she opened her mouth and said: '*Ciao, Stephanie!*' my insides turned to mush.

There was charisma, even star quality, as if Elizabeth Taylor had come into the room. She was more gorgeous than the Ferrari Dino! I couldn't look away.

We put on our coats and went for a pizza. It was evening, and there were no other children there. Ilaria sat down, ate her Margarita and – here was where I lost all restraint in my admiration – drank out of a glass. I gazed helplessly at her until it was time to leave.

All I could think, all the way home, was: *How can I get one of those?*

Clearly, there was a problem. Though I may look and sound as though I could be from Italy, I've never even lived there. Therefore having Italian children would have meant probably moving there or at least sleeping with an Italian man, which would have confused the issue – literally, since Peter was a half-Welsh Yorkshireman. Should I dump him and go on a mission to Rome? A bad idea, as I had a dodgy track record in this area. This dated back to a school trip to Pompeii, when I attempted to have sex in a Fiat. It was a Cinquecento – tiny even by Italian standards – and the guy was *tall*; for us to engage conclusively would have meant his legs sticking out the window, which might have caught the attention of the Latin teachers. So even though I had nothing actually against Italian men – and loved their cars, even the small ones – I knew the case for geographical engineering was weak. And even if it hadn't been, I just didn't see myself moving to a country where they served meat without vegetables and changed governments once a week.

But there was yet *another* obstacle. Even if I could find a way of having an Italian child in Britain, with a half-Welsh Yorkshireman, I didn't like the accessories. Being marketed very efficiently, the props were high profile. If you didn't ski, there was no reason to know what ski-sticks looked like. But baby gear you couldn't avoid. Even if the nearest you got to children was getting a lift back from a party in someone else's car, you'd never forget how long it took them to unhook the special seats.

'Hang on a sec, I'll just do the back for you . . . Nigel, could you grab the thing, and pull it down? I can't reach.'

'Just unclip the thing under the other thing.'

'I am.'

'No, no, the *other* thing—'

'Ow!'

It was easier to reconfigure the interior of a 747. And because of their ubiquity, I was convinced that you had to order children *with* certain things, as from a set menu. And they were all things I didn't like, for example puppet shows, and clowns, and teddy wallpaper, and group singing, particularly with *clapping*, and birthday napkins with smiley faces on them, and those slimy party bags that feel like condoms, and snot. I didn't like cot bumpers or child seats that make your perfectly nice car suddenly look like a Wendy house, or cups that you could tip upside-down but which didn't go with anything because for some reason they had to be *orange*. Nor could I stand to see grown women putting their purses in bags which were quilted and covered with *rabbits*. What, they were no longer allowed anything smart? And why couldn't they have *corners*? Suddenly their world was a padded cell? When I saw them pushing those prams with the matching changing bags I wanted to scream. Other people appeared to have all this paraphernalia, and more amazingly, to like it. And some, to my horror, even downgraded themselves as well. How could women refer to themselves – with a simpering smile – as *'Just a mum!'* as if that meant they ought to have their credit cards taken away and no longer be allowed to vote.

My encounter with Ilaria had changed me, but it only served to plunge me deeper into my dilemma. I was afraid that if I wasn't vigilant, whatever had happened to my parents would happen to me. They had got married and divorced, so I'd better not get married. They had split up and made me commute between them, so I shouldn't have children because they would end up torn in two. If my parents, who weren't actually mad or cruel or negligent, produced someone as hopeless as *me*, then *my* children would have to be total head-cases. It was a kind of formula: marriage + children = emotional melt-down. So I had cleverly protected myself from it by always making sure I ended up single, lonely and miserable. As formulas go, it was crap. Even after meeting Peter and wrecking the 'single' part of it, I clung to the other part by picking an argument whenever he mentioned marriage. I was so blinkered I hadn't even worked out that if I *did* marry someone stable, I could counteract the effect – or that marrying the right man might make me happier. And I certainly never thought that motherhood itself might bring me any pleasure. As for the outlandish possibility that *I* might bring something good to the equation – it just never occurred to me.

Clearly, then, motherhood was a faraway place of which I knew nothing. The destination and the journey were too hazardous. I would have to remain behind at Base Camp, in charge of something easy, like tidying the maps. When the real explorers came in, I'd be relieved to be out of the blizzard, but perpetually ever so slightly angry with myself for having given into my fears. Oh, and there was one more thing. I'd always supported the *principle* of breastfeeding, but of the breasts themselves I was proprietorial. I really didn't want people sucking them unless I was 100 per cent totally in the mood.

2 The Thin Blue Line

Finally, curiosity gets the better of me. Despite the inhospitable mental conditions – can my body actually grow a *real, live BABY*? There's only one way to find out.

'With all this talk about will we, won't we, let's not forget to have sex!'

'Ha-ha!'

I miss a period, and when it seems unlikely that I'll be having the next one, Peter and I go to the Margaret Pyke Centre, central London's home of family planning, to have a test.

'Let's get one from the chemist,' he says at first.

'I don't trust them.' I just don't accept that you can establish something so *massive*, so Life and Death *major*, using a product bought in a shop. If there's a nurse in the room, I'll be more inclined to believe it.

The Margaret Pyke has just relocated to trendy Charlotte Street, amongst the wine bars, but I rather miss the old building, in the last seedy bit of Soho, behind the apocalyptic-looking Soho Women's Hospital; I liked going for my condoms to a place surrounded by used needles and retired prostitutes in slippers. To warn of the follies of unprotected sex, they had only to point out of the window.

A senior nurse takes my sample and we sit in suspense, the atmosphere strangely like that of a quiz show. *And the winner is . . .*

'You're pregnant,' she says with a smile. We must look stunned because she adds: 'And – you're happy about that?'

Oh, yes. With the *idea* of having a baby I'm ecstatic. But then, communism looked good on paper. If there is an actual person inside me, who is going to get bigger, it's going to have to Come Out. And I can't do it.

'We have a teensy bit of a problem,' I tell Peter. 'I can't do Natural Birth. In fact, I can't do Birth at all.'

'I'd have it for you, you know.'

He would too. He is that rare thing, a man who knows no medical fear. When his dodgy kidney was removed, he asked if he could *watch*. And he still has things done to his teeth – thanks to a cycling accident when he was eighteen – that make *Marathon Man* look like Winnie the Pooh.

'It's so unfair,' I say. 'You're the brave one.' He puts his hands on my shoulders.

'I'll back you totally,' he says, 'and do anything you want, except grow a beard and be in an active birth video.'

'If only I was the man.'

'Well, you are half-man.'

'What, you mean I hate chatting on the phone and can read maps?'

'No, that hormone thing.'

'Oh, *testosterone*.' It's true, I do have too much of it; it goes with having polycystic ovaries and a hairy upper lip. If it wasn't for electrolysis I'd look like Tom Selleck. In fact, since my hair's been going grey I've dreaded being stranded on a desert island, because without my hair dye and tweezers, I'd be unrecognizable. If it took them more than three months to rescue me, I'd look like Einstein. On the upside, though, if I ever become a war correspondent and get taken hostage, I could just wait for the transformation, and – disguised as a poor holy man – escape.

Peter points at me in what he thinks is an amusing way.

'You have got one orifice in your body that would probably be big enough.'

'My mouth? Oh, fuck off.'

The baby'll just have to stay in. Maybe I can make it hang on until, say, it's ready to go to work, and then we can negotiate it out, like a mad gunman. Except then it'll be a lot bigger. But at least I'll be able to reason with it. Perhaps, as with moving a piano, I can say, '*Can you twist to the left a bit?*' and, '*Watch that corner on the landing, that's my perineum.*' Or if all else fails: '*Here's a scalpel – can you cut off your shoulders?*'

What am I going to do?

I could start smoking again, I suppose. But even a very small baby will be too big for me. Besides, managing to give up fags was one of my few triumphs; I don't want to go through that eat-loads-of-crap-and-put-on-a-stone thing again.

What other options do I have? Well, let me see. If I were a man – a man who isn't Peter – would I be queuing up to do this?

'Men dash off to do things like climb mountains and freeze to death in the Antarctic because they can't have babies,' my mother's always said, and I used to think: *Oh, blah.* But now I'm beginning to see she has a point. If you'd had a third-degree tear like my friend Harriet, you wouldn't need to go up a mountain. You could say, *I have touched the fucking void, mate. In fact, my void is a bloody sight bigger than it used to be, thank you very much.* Given the choice, I'd rather crawl across the Andes with a broken leg than tear my – I can't even say it – *naughty bits.* Can you believe I used to write about sex in *Cosmopolitan*? I've led a double life, only the other way round from most people. Usually it's, *'Vicar was secret cross-dresser'* or *'Headmaster's wife posed nude in magazine.'* With me it's *'Fearless sex writer was secret prude.'* I did the first *'What Women Really Want In Bed'* piece for *GQ,* but I can't say the c-word. Unless it's *'Can* you not press so hard, please?'

I've got to *focus.* I've set a bomb ticking inside me, which cannot be defused. Or, as Cecil Parkinson memorably put it, *'You cannot put the toothpaste back in the tube.'* You can bet if *he* could have got pregnant he would have stayed in a lot more. Use the barrier method, Cecil: shut the front door.

'As far as I can see,' says Peter, 'it's very like buying a car.'

'If you're not going to say anything useful, could you shut up?'

'You study all the specifications, and then you make your choice . . . So, Ms Calman, what can I interest you in? We have the Sport Pack, with hard suspension, which keeps you in touch with every twist, turn and bump of the road. A *Real* Driving Experience. Or there's the Super Comfort Fully-Automatic model with cruise control, air suspension and a choice of six entertainment sources which lets you glide along in style and peace, ensuring that you arrive at parenthood relaxed and refreshed, ready to get on with the next phase of your life.'

'Yeah, well actually—'

It's no good; he's warming to his theme.

'Or perhaps you'd prefer the DIY experience? We send you the instructions and some components, and you put the whole thing together in your very own garage! You might rip some of your skin off with the wrench, but it's character forming!'

'I don't want to be pathetic, I just—'

'You're not pathetic. Look: imagine you're choosing a holiday. Camp on primitive site with basic facilities, or recline in five-star hotel?'

He knows I hate camping.

'Do you feel that without the feel of the ground next to your skin, the queue for the showers – you won't really have *travelled*?'

'It's not the same thing at all.'

'Yes, it is. You're prepared to spend more in the interests of comfort, right? You'd rather have a Jaguar than a Vectra.'

'Sure. If I'm going to crash, I like to do it on leather seats.'

I feel that, as we both love talking about cars, we have rather got away from the point.

He gestures at an article about elective Caesareans, at which the paper just happens to have fallen open.

'So there you go.'

'Where?'

'Queen Thingy's.'

It's true. I have been reading about an obstetrician at Queen Charlotte's Hospital who is quoted as being Pro-Choice.

'So ring him up.'

'What would I say? I'm not sure—'

'Start with: "How much?"'

So I do.

A helpful nurse answers and says:

'Well, with the surgeon ... anaesthetist ... and depending on, let's say, five nights' stay: four thousand pounds.'

'Right ...'

'That's without any extras, of course, like—'

'Bandages.'

'Ha-ha! No – meals.'

I get off the phone.

'You're right. It is like buying a car.'

After a few fruitless discussions about how we might obtain £4,000, Peter says, 'Why don't you talk to that doctor you like? See if she's got any ideas?'

'What, like: "*If you're so phobic, try not getting pregnant in the first place*"?'

'Negativity: that always helps.'

I go back to the Margaret Pyke Centre to see Doctor

Green. She has a slow, laconic delivery and slightly spacey smile, a bit like the Mona Lisa on Valium. But the content varies considerably from the presentation. She is shockingly candid, with that brutal humour you look for in a medic. Her idea of small talk is to chat about large-scale outbreaks of death. We open with that day's headlines: the women who have recently been found to have cervical cancer, despite getting negative smear test results. She says: 'Well, it's very boring reading cytology slides all day long. One's bound to make mistakes.' She admits she may also have said this to *Breakfast News*.

'Christ! You didn't, did you?'

'It was very early in the morning.'

'I need to ask you about, um, having a baby,' I say.

'Ah!' she says, the smile widening. 'You want to get pregnant?'

'I already am,' I say. 'It only took five weeks.'

'Goodness! So much for the polycystic ovaries!'

'So much indeed. They told me here I probably couldn't get pregnant.'

'Oh, what do they know? Well, you know you can't come and see me any more? I'm only Family Planning.'

'And I've Planned. But I need your help. What do you do . . .' I say, 'if you sort of do want to have a baby – but are too scared to actually have one?'

'Well . . .'

'I'm *petrified*. What am I going to do?!'

'Do you want to know,' she says soothingly, 'who all my doctor friends go to?'

Do I?

'Mr Silverstone. Like the racetrack. He's The One.'

'Is it – is he – you know, really expensive?'

'NHS. Get your GP to refer you. You won't get a free Caesarean out of him, though.'

'Never mind. I'll save up. Thank you! How many children do you have, by the way? I've never asked.'

'Oh, I don't have children,' she says. 'I have cats.' And she does that smile again.

To celebrate our last few months of Freedom, we book a holiday in Tobago. While I'm combing through my wardrobe for something to pose in on the beach, Peter is doing research amongst his female acquaintance.

'Hey, look, I've finally got a reason not to wear a bikini. I've always had a wobbly tummy and now it's OK!'

'Excellent. Definitely worth getting pregnant for.'

'Yeah! Isn't it great? Look at this.' I try to swan across the room, but tie my sarong too tight, so that I walk like a bad imitation of a penguin.

'Marie says we have to get a Nuchal Fold Scan.' Marie is his deputy at work, mother of two girls.

'What is *that*?'

'I have no idea.'

'Very useful.'

'Hang on, I've got something else here, from Julia.'

Julia, one of his old school friends, is about to have baby number four. She combines immense efficiency with a kind of vague breeziness, a cross between Joyce Grenfell and Annie Hall.

'She says go to Kypros Nicolaides.'

'And that would be where?'

'I dunno. Wait, yes I do.' He fiddles around with his yellow stickies. 'The Fetal Medicine Centre.'

From being completely in the dark – the obstetric equivalent of a remote tribe who've never seen a camera – we suddenly become experts.

The Nuchal Fold Scan is £80. Apparently there are two types of test: the scary, needle-in-the tummy kind which include CVS and amniocentesis, and the easy-peasy, blood test plus ultrasound scan, which this one is. The blood tests have funny names: the Double Test, The Barts, the Leeds, the Triple. And they offer odds: 1 in 1000; 1 in 200; 1 in 10.

'They sound like horse races,' says Peter. 'What does it all mean?'

'It means your risk factor of having a Down's syndrome baby,' explains the rational but friendly female doctor at the Centre. 'We measure the fold of skin at the back of the baby's neck; it's the best indicator we've yet found for Down's.'

'But it's not an absolute Yes or No?'

'No, but the blood test is very accurate, and we don't do one without the other. You'll know a lot more than with the NHS tests, and far sooner.'

'So we could be out of the woods, as it were, by—'

'Thirteen weeks.'

'What, no amnio? No potentially bad news at twenty weeks?'

'Hopefully not. If you *do* get a high risk factor, we can offer you the CVS, or Chorionic Villus Sampling which, unlike the amnio, tests the actual cells in the placenta, as opposed to the fluid.'

'So if you *do* terminate—'

'It's much earlier.'

'And therefore much less horrible. So why don't all the hospitals offer this?'

'It's quite specialized. You can't just bung in a machine and let them get on with it.'

'And when can we do this?'

'Eleven weeks. Obviously, we discuss it with you at all stages.'

'Eighty quid for peace of mind?' says Peter. 'A bargain.'

At ten weeks we go and see my GP, who says he's never heard of the CVS and anyway there's no point asking him anything because the real expert is the community midwife. Can we book an ultrasound scan? No. Would he like to take my blood pressure? No. Shall we – play Scrabble? His lack of interest is slightly embarrassing, as if this is a car showroom and not a surgery at all. But we have to be friends with him because we need the referral.

At eleven weeks the community midwife waves away questions about such trivia as the baby to concentrate on something really important: geography. Apparently we live on a fault line between catchment areas so I have to change midwife teams after the birth.

'You live in Islington South, but after the birth you'd have to be cared for by a team from Islington *North*.' Clearly this is a Big Deal. Are Islington North and South at war? I've been so preoccupied, there's probably a lot I don't know. We try to drag the conversation back to the pregnancy.

'I really want to arrange a scan. I am thirty-six, after all, and well – I really want to see the baby. It could be a hysterical pregnancy – or wind!' I'm sending up my own anxiety here: give me a break! She doesn't smile.

'OK, what about this CVS?' says Peter. 'Should we be thinking about that?'

'Oh, you're too late for that.' (This is *not true*.)

Eventually – with forceps – we extract a leaflet from her about tests for Down's syndrome and other conditions.

'Can we at least *arrange* the scan? We're going on holiday at the end of the week.'

'Plenty of time. You'll get a hospital appointment in – ooh, two or three weeks.'

In other words, when it's too late. We are dealing with parallel universes. We don't have strong views about NHS or private; we just want them to recognize that to us, this banal little event is *important*.

'It'll be fine,' says Peter, deploying the phrase that over the coming months, will make me want to hit him with a pan.

In Tobago we watch families playing in the sea together, and crocodiles of beautifully turned out schoolchildren who say, 'Good morning!' to the ladies who sit outside their shops.

'Look! Look!' I say. 'Listen!'

'You sound like an Early Reading Book.'

'I like the school uniform.'

'Yeah. Just one thing. We don't actually live here.'

'Be nice, though.'

'Yeah . . . everyone's so polite.'

'Can we have polite children in blue pinafores?'

'Don't they still use the cane? Isn't that why they're so well behaved?'

'Well, they look good anyway.'

On the second night, the hotel has '2 for 1' at the bar.

'I think you can have *one*,' he says.

'Oh, thanks! Is it going to be like this from now on?'

'Like what? You're pregnant, for God's sake.'

'One pina colada, please.'

The bar lady puts down two foamy white glasses.

'Oh thanks, but I only wanted *one*.'

'Ah, but it's 2 for 1, you see?'

It goes down amazingly fast.

'Actually, they're not that strong, are they? Mostly pineapple and coconut.'

'Well, bars always do that, water them down. They're hardly going to use double measures of rum in a promotion.'

We have four each.

In the night I wake up and remember that just before Christmas, I went out with two girls from work and had a *lot* of wine. And of course I was already pregnant by about three or four weeks. So the damage is done anyway, but it's not my fault because I didn't know. This is a huge relief, and I go back to sleep.

*

At thirteen weeks we're back. I ring the hospital to check that the GP has done the referral, and they've never heard of me.

'What are we going to do? I'm supposed to be in the system!'

Peter says: 'It'll be fine.'

'But they said I don't exist!'

'It'll be fine.'

'Go away before I hurt you.'

Meanwhile we go to the Fetal Medicine Centre for the Nuchal Fold Scan. As on the phone, we pepper the doctor with questions, and again she stands up to the pressure rather well.

She puts the cold jelly on my stomach and turns the monitor to show us a grainy black and white film. It reminds me a bit of when I was eight, and we stayed up to watch man's first step on the moon.

'That bean-shaped thing, floating there in space . . .'

'Is your baby inside you, yes.'

My God: it's really there.

'It just seems so – unlikely!'

I so wasn't going to have children that for a moment I wonder if this is a video they keep for fantasists. I'm glad Peter is in the room; people won't be able to say I've imagined it – except they won't say that anyway, because to everyone else this is *completely normal*, whereas for me it's like Galileo telling the Vatican that the earth went round the sun. *Are you saying there is a Live Person inside my Body? Whom I haven't even met?* It must be witchcraft.

We take our scan photo, and go for coffee.

'There's a person inside your tummy,' says Peter.

'Oh my God!' I say. 'Bloody Hell!!!'

'Give it a nice shot of caffeine, there you go. Help it bounce around a bit more. And have a cake. You're eating for two now.'

I have an éclair, and some toast, and finish his strudel as well.

'I said eating for two, not six.'

I kiss him goodbye and go for a swim. When I get there, it's Special Needs Day, and everyone in the changing room has Down's syndrome. What are the odds on *that*?

Afterwards I get back on the phone to University College Hospital. Have they got my referral from the surgery?

'No. Sorry,' says the woman.

'What can I do?'

'Well . . . we don't normally tell people this, but you can self-refer.' Bastards! I knew they were concealing something.

I get the surgery to fax the letter they should have sent in the first place, and I'm in.

The receptionist in the UCH antenatal department is a glamorous black girl who looks as though she should be processing nightclub tickets, not patient notes. Her stylishness lifts the ambience of the whole place. She memorizes my name on this first occasion, and remembers it ever afterwards. How do people do that? Probably by not drinking four pina coladas.

After all the questions about family illnesses, and taking my blood pressure, and after I've weed all over one of those tiny little pots, the midwife asks me how much alcohol I drink. People always lie about this, I bet. I'll be really honest, that'll impress her.

'Ooh, about . . . twenty-eight units a week. Three to four glasses a day.'

'Let's just put down one glass of wine a day, shall we?'

She looks at me as if to say: *'I'm doing you a big favour, you alcoholic old tart.'* Why don't you just come out with it? *'Poisons fetus with entire contents of Oddbins.'* Put that on your bloody form. I decide not to mention the 2 for 1 pina coladas.

Anyhow, you have to drink *loads* to give them Fetal Alcohol Syndrome. My friend Kirsty's sister, who's a midwife, says you can tell the ones who've got it – whose mothers drank a lot when they were pregnant – because their heads are sort of oval. And in fact I have seen one quite recently, walking past Somerfield. She was really weird-looking, a grown-up, about thirty. Her face was sort of pointy; eyes almost round the side instead of the front. Either that, or Somerfield is being used a landing base for aliens. Yep, I thought: that's a bit more than four pina coladas. Which were mostly pineapple and coconut, by the way – did I mention that?

Leaving the house one evening, I am accosted – there is no other word for it – by the American woman renting the house next door. She looks at my tummy, and at the bottle of wine I'm taking to a dinner party, and gasps melodramatically.

'What?' I say. 'What's the matter?'

'Look!' she says. 'You can't – take THAT!'

'What, the wine?' Is she serious? She is. 'It's all right,' I explain slowly. 'In England we can do this.' And in my head I add the three little words: *Now fuck off.*

It goes with all the other things I'm not supposed to do any more, including eating curry and soft cheese, not eating, running, climbing, arguing, going on escalators, slapping people, shouting, looking at pictures of George Clooney and getting stressed.

But I've got an important matter to attend to. It's daunting, but once you're pregnant it simply has to be done. And it's no good putting it off, either: my breasts are about to get Bigger. How Much Bigger, my friends warn me, I can't possibly imagine. They also tell me that their dimensions, like the value of all endowments, can go down as well as up; I could end up, after breastfeeding, with less than I started with. Well, I can't help that. For the present I need something that will (a) make sure they don't sag, even for a second, and (b) in four months' time prevent them from knocking people over in lifts. The last piece of underwear I had professional *involvement* in, was my black lace wedding basque. I went to Selfridge's and had to bend over to 'fill the cups correctly'. But I didn't mind because it looked *fantastic*. I took it home, lay on the bed and pretended to be Elizabeth Taylor in *Cat on a Hot Tin Roof*, only not married to a homosexual alcoholic.

'I have to get a bra fitted,' I tell Peter. As the co-perp, he has to be informed of everything I do, think or feel for the next six months. 'But I don't much fancy the thought of a stranger, you know, seeing my tits.'

'Can't you just buy one? Go in like the SAS? Grab a couple and run.' This is his solution to the agony of shopping. He has to return quite a lot of things.

'You mean deploy the ancient Navajo method of screwing up the eyes and guessing?'

'The label on this says you're a ninety-six. Blimey, I didn't know you were that big. I quite fancy you now.'

'That's centimetres, you fuckwit.'

'Oh.' He looks crestfallen, then brightens. 'If I'd known bras would play such a key role, I'd have got someone pregnant before.'

Shortly afterwards I get down to the lingerie department of a well-known department store. The normal underwear looks even tinier than usual, which must be the Alice in Wonderland effect; I have eaten the cake of conception and am about to become Huge. Nonetheless the flimsy strings of lace on the racks do not depress me; I have been assured by everyone that breastfeeding will ping my figure back to its previous tautness, the only problem being that I haven't actually been taut since I was about ten. By fourteen I already had a stomach that when I ran, jogged up and down like a chicken in a carrier bag. And every pound I've ever put on since has gone straight to it. Now it's three chickens. Still! At least now I've got an excuse. And there does seem to be a good choice of the 'fuller' models on show.

I grab a couple of nice ones to try on while I wait for the assistant. And that's when I notice the old model, that I've been meaning to replace for a while. Bra years are definitely longer; this one I've had for – well, it doesn't *seem* that long, and is no longer white and shapely but bizarrely stretched, thin and grey, like an elephant's scrotum. I drop it on the seat and it seems to shrivel, like the witch's feet in *The Wizard of Oz*.

Mmm, though! The new one is WHITE and crisp and even, like mass-produced meringue. The cups are so firm my tits are now bashing my chin, but the lace makes me feel a bit gorgeous. I can imagine Peter murmuring speechlessly, perhaps coming into the bedroom behind me and saying, '*Fuck! How much did that cost, then?*'

Anyway, I look at myself from all the angles in the mirrors, ring the bell and wait. Then, during the wait, I lose heart. My *joie de vivre* evaporates, and I become suffused with a mixture of shame and anxiety that gives way to foreboding. Standing half-clothed in a cubicle, under a merciless white light, makes me feel like the victim of something nameless and medical. This feeling gets such a grip on me that by the time the assistant comes in, I'm sure she's going to tell me I've got six months to live.

The sales floor is full of lovely, satiny, lacy things, in marvellous colours, but all the ones she's brought are utilitarian and devoid of flounce – like how you'd imagine a government bra designed for prisons. Is it because I'm pregnant, or because I look as if I've had too much fun in my life? Does she think I need taking down a peg or two? I feel suddenly very small and vulnerable, like a refugee about to be deloused.

'You won't be able to wear that.'

'Why not?'

'You can't wear underwired when you're pregnant.' Why? Does the wire transmit subversive messages to the fetus? There's a conspiracy here to make me be ugly, I know it.

'As you get bigger, it compresses the top of your tummy.'

'Oh.' My tummy's not going to be up HERE! (It is, of course.) I put on one of the others. She stares at me, and with the expression surveyors adopt when confronted by subsidence, sinks into a morose silence. Eventually she says: 'How's that for you?' in the tone a hangman might use about his rope. Two more, Amish-type bras are tried on.

'And when do I get the – nursing one?'

'Well, obviously not now!'

'No, of course.' *How stupid.*

'You have to come back – when you're bigger.'

'Right. Right.' How soon can I get out of here? I attempt to hide the scrotum under my bag, but she spots it and, like a health inspector, pronounces it condemned.

'Well, that one's totally gone.'

'Oh, I know!' Why do I want her *approval*?

'Do you handwash your bras? You should, you know.'

'Yes, yes, of course, I will, I promise,' I babble, desperate to return to a society where I am no longer a number in a cubicle but a free woman. Somehow, I manage to display a bit of spine and take, along with the bra for offenders, one in black shiny satin. It's in the sports range, but I fearlessly break the rules and demand they take my £21.

I tell Peter: 'I'm never going into another cubicle, I'll tell you that.'

'How are you going to vote?' (It is May 1997.)

'Do pregnant women have the vote?'

'And anyway, won't you have to go back again when your tits get *really* huge?'

'Well! As you weren't there to support me, you have to come and do the next stage.'

'Er . . .'

Things have improved hugely since, but not that many years ago maternity clothes were still like punishments devised by some extreme seventeenth-century sect. They seemed to symbolize the loss of not only your figure but your whole adult identity, managing to make you look like both a baby and an old maid at the same time, the sort of woman whose elderly parents still choose her clothes.

The main style on offer is a kind of Midwestern

Vernacular: huge smocks, drawstring skirts like shower curtains, and trousers with expanding panels in the front. Everything is *checked*. You can have white with blue checks, or blue with white checks. I haven't worn any kind of pinafore since primary school, and they don't bring back great memories. All I need to complete the ambience would be a bottle of scent made from disinfectant, over-cooked cabbage and off milk. If I was going to play Anne of Green Gables on children's television in Romania, I might, just might, wear this. But what's this? All-in-one *playsuits*? I'm having a baby, not trying to dress like one.

A few yards away Peter is making sicky faces.

'*Dungarees* – yeuch! You know how I feel about dungarees.'

'Well, move away from them, then.' I'm not even a mother yet, and already our relationship has changed. 'And stop being *silly*.'

'You can't wear *any* of these: you'll look like a kanga-roo. It's lucky we've already had sex. Because there is *no way* . . .'

'Yeah, all right. I've got to wear *something*.'

These garments not only make you look as though you aren't having sex now, but as if you never had any in the first place. It's what you'd imagine might happen if the entire fashion business were taken over by Mormons. I can only assume there's a chip in the software of maternity-wear designers that programmes them to consider you spent. You've been impregnated, therefore do not need to attract the opposite sex ever again. And there's certainly no room for the crazy notion of wanting to look nice for *yourself*.

Eventually we do find some semi-tolerable outfits, but they're in the shops with the loudest music, staffed by girls who become baffled when confronted by numerals larger than 10. Ask for anything over a 12, and they just run away. I saw a pregnant Barbie once – the baby and tummy 'casing' snapped on and off – and these drainpipe trousers with slightly elasticated fronts were evidently designed for her. Either that, or for anorexics, the latter not being generally noted for their fertility. Perhaps we've missed a sign saying *Maternity Dept – Age 9–12*.

We break for lunch. That I'm good at.

'I could always try the catalogues. There's one called *Blooming Marvellous*.'

'Why?'

'So British, isn't it? I'm feeling Blooming Marvellous. I eat fifteen meals a day, and I wee all the time – sometimes even in a toilet – but I'm feeling Blooming Marvellous!'

'Try Fucking Enormous,' says Peter. He puts on an smarmy voice. *'Fucking Enormous, can I help you?'*

'Yeah, you can: order me a glass of red wine.'

Spring has sprung. We go for the twenty-week scan.

'It's got a Big Head,' says the radiographer.

'A big brain, you mean? Ha-ha!'

'No, just a Big Head. And a short femur.'

'Christ, it's a Calman all right.'

'It's amazing the detail they can see by now.'

'I know. Any hair on the legs?'

After this, Julia rings up again, to recommend a chic French maternity shop near Bond Street.

'It sounds expensive, but you'll only need to get one or two things. I wore the same skirt for *months*. Also, with their stuff you won't feel like such a lump.'

'Thanks. No, really.'

'Wait till you're like a house,' she says. 'And you think *I can't get any bigger than this: it's not possible*. Then look at the calendar.'

'Why?'

'Because you'll have another two months to go.'

*

Then a few weeks later, a friend of ours gets married. And I find this – gown. In *Wallis*. It's stretchy, with a sort of bronzy-coloured snake-pattern. It feels all slinky and springy and not at all blob-like. I try it on, and severely fancy myself. It does bring to mind this book I had as a child, in which a snake swallows a live mongoose, but I don't care. Besides no one else seems to have read it. I go to the wedding and everyone says, '*Wow!*', I think in a good way. When I get up to make my Best Woman speech, though, I have trouble squeezing between the tables.

'I've got that condition that's the opposite of anorexia.'

'Eh?'

'You think you're quite slim, but in fact you're really fat.'

'You're not fat, you're pregnant.'

'Yeah? Well, you started it.'

3 Babies *Do* Come Out of Mummy's Tummy

Summer is approaching. I have to grasp, as it were, the birth nettle. We arrange to go and see Mr Silverstone.

'He is completely wonderful,' says Julia. 'So nice you just want to go back and have more.'

Mr S gives women the choice of natural delivery for subsequent babies following a C-section, which is rare. He also, I discover, departs from the conventional wisdom that women too frightened to give birth normally are vain, pathetic time-wasters who should be pelted with boiling vodka and wear a bib embroidered with a 'C' of shame.

'Remember,' says Peter, on our way in. 'You don't have to justify yourself.'

'Four thousand pounds, remember?'

'I think you should definitely justify yourself.'

I put on my grooved orange top from the French shop that makes me look like a pumpkin. Mr Silverstone is a consultant, and consultants are protected by layers of nurses, house officers and registrars to keep the likes of us away. Yes, we have been referred to him, but as anyone who's ever tried to see their consultant knows, they're like celebrity chefs. Their names are on the menus, but when you go to their restaurants, they're never the ones cooking the actual food.

'I've got some – issues to discuss,' I explain to each nurse, midwife and doctor. 'And I'm only going to discuss them with him.'

Mr Silverstone inhabits a small room at University College Hospital, London. Thin and smartly dressed, in a blue cotton shirt and tie, he exhibits the neat, modest movements of someone who doesn't need to draw attention to himself. There's none of the swagger traditionally associated with consultants. The nurses do not back away like geishas when he comes down the corridor. He talks to his staff quietly and courteously. He's not unique in medicine by any means, but he stands out.

The minute we sit down together, I feel more optimistic and I can tell Peter does too. After all, if I fall to bits or go off my trolley, he's the one who'll be left holding the offspring. The atmosphere is pleasantly civilized, as if we might be equals. Indeed, he gives the impression that rather than a whole person escaping from my nether regions, we could be discussing something more aesthetically enriching, like a new kitchen.

I describe my fears, and wait for him to tell me to pull myself together.

He clasps his hands together between his knees, and leans forward. He has been listening so intensely that for a moment the whole infrastructure – room, building, city – seems to fade away. There is nothing else there except – well, it feels a bit like love. Afterwards I remember that Sigmund Freud is said to have listened like that, in a way that caused his patients to proclaim that they had never been listened to so completely in their lives. He says: 'Have you considered a Caesarean section?'

I have gone in, not knowing how to face the biggest fear of my life, and come out feeling – *allowed*. I consider starting a cult to worship him.

We have extra drinks that night to celebrate. We're meeting Ray and Sarah, some old friends, who are going to have a baby at around the same time. We'll have so much to talk about!

We sit down in the restaurant, and as soon as we mention our triumphant visit to Mr S, we're in trouble.

'You do realize,' says Ray, 'that having an epidural harms the baby?'

'Don't be ridiculous,' I say.

'And so does pethidine. All pain relief, in fact.'

This is our first experience of Men Who Don't Believe

in Relief For a Pain They Won't Be Having – and it's fascinating.

'Would you have, say, a circumcision without an anaesthetic?' I ask him.

'That's so bloody stupid!' he snarls.

Sarah and I look at each other.

'What are you planning to do?'

'I'll just leave it to the doctors,' she says.

'Well . . . they don't *always* know best,' I venture. I am thinking of a friend who was told '*Your baby's dead*' after the lead of the fetal heart monitor had fallen off.

'Are you saying you know better than *doctors?*'

'Well, these days midwives are more—'

'This is just stupid,' says Ray again. Peter attempts to lighten the mood.

'A bloke at work told me he was standing outside the delivery room listening to this terrible screaming, and he said to the bloke next to him, '*Bloody hell! Listen to that!*' And the bloke said, '*We're not having pain relief.*'

We walk home in silence, which is particularly tricky because they're staying with us.

Over the next few months, we have extensive experience of the Moral Hierarchy of Birth Methods, with – naturally – No Pain Relief at the top. Before you read on, though – or email me – please just note one thing. I have nothing but admiration for women who give birth the way nature intended, and if I ever thought there was the slightest hope of my doing so, I would. But I know myself, and I'm not one of them. Even my mother, former press officer of the National Childbirth Trust and potentially the most annoying person I could possibly meet at this stage – upon hearing my absolute terror of childbirth, extends her sympathy and support. With that in mind, I must say, it is easier to go on. Still, I become a magnet for everyone's Birth Politics.

'I do personally favour a Caesarean,' says a woman from Peter's work. 'But I wouldn't have one, because if you don't actually give birth, your body fails to release oxytocin and bonding doesn't occur.'

Which rather begs the question: if the Caesarean is an emergency, does bonding occur then?

I could do what Kate Winslet subsequently did – and lie. But I'm not an actress and lie badly. Besides, I am intrigued by how the choice I – an individual – make about my method of delivery, is taken to mean that I am anti every other method and therefore have to be taken to task. My C-section doesn't illustrate my attitude to natural births, any more than using a condom makes me anti-Pill. If you wear black to a party and I wear pink – does my pink automatically state that I believe black is *wrong*?

'Is home-made bread better than shop bought?' says Peter.

'Usually, yes, it is.'

'Ah, but is it *morally superior?*'

Confident that he has had the Last Word on the matter, he opens his car magazine. Well, at least one of us is going to be in good shape for the birth. I, on the other hand, come home every other day in a state because someone or other has 'picked on me' about my choice.

On top of which, I'm completely stressed at work. At thirty-seven weeks, I'm still on a project that should have finished by now, and am getting on so badly with one of the team that I keep thinking I'm going to have a heart attack and die.

'Well, that'd solve your Caesarean problem,' says Peter.

'The weeks leading up to the birth are supposed to be CALM!' I scream.

Maybe if I'd been a man, I might now be writing: *Week 37: I am continuing to produce excellent work. I am earning good money – and am soon to be a Mother as well!*

The day arrives. There are two surgeons, two anaesthetists, a couple of nurses and two more people as well. Are they training *everyone* in this theatre? Or am I so nervous I'm seeing double?

'What do you do?' I ask a bloke in theatre greens.

'I'm a Medical Technician.'

That makes eight. No wonder the NHS isn't keen. I try not to look at the row of scalpels. As I bend forward for the epidural, they ask me about the CD we've brought. Peter's choice of opera duets has won over mine of *James Brown Live at the Apollo*. Even though I know they're trying to distract me, I feel flattered. It makes a pleasant change from: *'Going on holiday this year?'* as they shove in a freezing speculum.

'I feel as though I'm at a cocktail party,' I say at one point.

'Oh yes,' says the anaesthetist, 'we like to provide that atmosphere.' Someone produces a bar, a bit like a huge loo-roll holder.

'You're not going to stick *that* in my back, are you?'

They hang a cloth over it, screening off what my sister refers to as your 'lower parts'.

'I know it sounds silly, but I hate taking my pants off. Can I keep them on?'

'Of course, darling,' says the nurse.

Julia has told me, *'You'll feel a sort of rummaging'*, but I don't feel even that. Suddenly two hands are holding a baby high in the air. It really was in there! Peter puts his hand to his mouth, tears in his eyes, and gasps: 'It's a boy!'

'It's Lawrence!'

'Dignity?! You won't have any of that,' crowed a male friend, whose wife had a long, horrific labour.

Well, Blah to you.

I've got away with it! A whole little boy has come out of me, and despite all my imperfections, he is absolutely fine. Well, almost.

Lawrence's breathing doesn't sound quite right. The paediatrician says he is 'grunting'. He looks fine, or as fine as a newborn baby can look, resembling the usual red prune. His weight is fine. But his blood isn't picking up enough oxygen.

Peter takes him to meet my mother and my sister. Someone pushes a Polaroid into my hand: a picture of a baby. A chill goes through me as I realize it's Lawrence. I shove it back at them; it makes it seem as though he is dead.

Peter takes a proper picture of us together, then Lawrence goes off to the Neonatal Unit, and he and I go back to the fifth floor. Thankfully, Lawrence isn't in the Intensive Care bit, which would be really scary, just the moderately scary Special Care Unit.

Eventually Peter goes away. too, and I spend the night sitting amongst all the other mothers – with their babies – in the Postnatal ward. It isn't at all traumatic,

if you count listening to six babies crying as not traumatic. It's intriguing, watching all these mothers looking
after their babies, feeding and changing them, cuddling
them and holding little, murmured conversations. Will I
be able to do all this? Although I've had my baby, I'm
still on a provisional licence.

Not having my baby with me seems quite normal; it
is, after all, my default mode. I don't feel that we've been
wrenched apart; I'm not used to the condition of motherhood, so it'll give me time to break myself in. After all,
he's not in danger. It's all part of the adventure. Besides,
when you're as nervous as I am, the full battery of
medicine's finest is a comfort. Being sent home in charge
of a helpless infant: *that's* scary.

I'm looking at a week of staying with these nice
people who won't make me wash up or get my own tea.
I have a bed up on the fifth floor, at the end by the
windows, with a view over the rooftops. Peter, Claire and
my mother bring in Danish pastries and coffee, the odd
sandwich and other essentials such as chocolate and,
later on, Indian takeaways and beer. I can receive friends
arriving with treats and flowers then, like a Victorian
mother, pop down to Neonatal twice a day for a spot of
Heritage Parenting. I sit amongst my bouquets and cards
and feel good. One fine afternoon, a friend and I go out

on the balcony with tea and biscuits, and sit in the warm air like two colonial ladies on their veranda. It is, all in all, quite a holiday.

My heart sinks, though, when I try to express milk. A grey, metal pump is wheeled in on a trolley, like an exhibit from the metereological display at the Science Museum: one of those early devices for measuring precipitation in the section that nobody looks at.

I clamp on the glass trumpet and listen to the growling sound of the machine. After half an hour's concerted pumping I have about ten millilitres, enough to fill the syringe at the top of Lawrence's tiny feeding tube only once. They ask if I will allow him to be given formula. What if I say: '*No, I'd rather he starved to death on ten millilitres, so long as it's my own*'? Will they go ahead and give it to him anyway? I appreciate their attempt to include me in the decision-making process. Every hour, I drop friends, tea and present-opening, and run down to the nursery to plug myself in. Despite the clearly inadequate nature of my offerings, no one says, '*Blimey! You don't think he's going to survive on that, do you?!*' Instead, they solemnly take the tiny plastic pot, with its almost invisible liquid in the bottom, and pour it into the tube.

*

At 7.30 on a Sunday morning, when Lawrence has been in Neonatal for all the four days of his life, I get up to go to the lavatory. In an hour or so Peter will arrive with my coffee and Danish and we'll visit him together. I am just making my way across the ward when I'm intercepted by a breathless Filipina ancillary.

'Have you heard the news?!' she cries.

The blood seems to drain from my head. This is it. All that stuff about a minor breathing problem was obviously a lie. Lawrence is all the way down in the basement. I can't get there in time! And anyway, it's clearly too late. They didn't even say he was that ill. I think, *what a way to tell me*. They could have at least sent a doctor.

In the two or three seconds before I can sputter out the word: *'Lawrence!'* she says: 'Princess *Di-a-na*!!'

I shake her. 'Lawrence? What's happened to *LAWRENCE?!!*'

'Princess *Di-a-na* has been killed!'

Why can't she stop babbling this rubbish and answer?

'Don't be ridiculous!' I say, and start for the lift.

Suddenly I realize that she isn't talking about Lawrence at all. I turn back and slap her – luckily not very hard, on the arm.

'I thought you meant my baby!! Oh, God – I'm sorry!'

She shrugs and smiles, and goes off to repeat this silly hoax about the Princess.

When I get down to the nursery, all the little radios are on as usual, but instead of pop music they're playing the National Anthem. Weird! And some of the nurses are sort of standing to attention.

'Lawrence! Lawrence!'

'Sssh!'

I reach the incubator. He is fine. I can't believe they're thinking about anything else.

4 How Many Breastfeeding Women Does It Take to Change a Lightbulb?

Visiting our baby is like gaining access to a safety deposit box. The Special Care Unit is down in the basement, like a vault. We have to ask, and – if the nurses are busy helping someone else – wait. Then he has to be held a bit carefully so as not to pull off his wires. But though he's technically ours, the hospital has control. It's like Monet's *Waterlilies*; it belongs to the nation, but you just try putting it in your bag to take home. When the doctors do their rounds, we have to wait outside. Even though we understand this, Peter says afterwards: 'It's as if we shouldn't be here.'

A young midwife called Karen hands me a book called *Kangaroo Care*.

'It's about the benefits to babies of being held against the human body,' she explains, 'when they're sick or premature or even just like Lawrence – nearly well.'

I read it, and rush down to the Unit. With Karen at my side, I open my nightie and cuddle Lawrence and feel the first glimmerings of confidence. Hey, this is *great*! Peter has a go. We go back to the ward in triumph.

The next day, I can't wait to try again. Karen isn't on, and Peter hasn't arrived yet. So I go down alone. But instead of the nurses I know, there's a different one. I ask to take him out of the incubator.

'You'll have to wait. I've got paperwork to do.'

Her brisk, forbidding tone suggests I have no right.

Paperwork? *Paperwork?!* Perhaps she's right. What do I know? I wait. Then I wait some more. Altogether I stand in front of that plastic box for *forty-five minutes*. It feels like forty-five hours. I become aware of a mounting urge to grab the nurse and shove her head very hard against the wall. Instead, I keep asking politely while she finds more and yet more other things to do. She then goes on her break, leaving me standing in front of the incubator, tears streaming down my face.

The next nurse comes on.

'Are you OK?' she says.

Moments later I feel Lawrence in my arms. What *was* that? It wasn't like love, it was like having my drink spiked. When I envisaged injuring the horrible nurse, the image bypassed the rational '*Shall I do this?*' process, the little debate you have with yourself before you, for example, shout '*Fuck Off*' at a policeman. I am not in control here. I've been taken over by some kind of – force – like with Captain Kirk and the crew of the Enterprise when they were taken over by aliens who controlled them with invisible, low-budget telepathy. But by the end of the episode they were always in charge of themselves again. Am I always going to be like this? Can't I switch it *off*? Uh-oh. *This* is what the fuss is about. *This* is Maternal Instinct.

No wonder I didn't recognize it! I expected it to be *nice*. And I'm stuck with it. Like a virus it's now in my system and – whenever it chooses, can *come back*? I suddenly realize the bargain I've made. I haven't just 'had a baby'. I've created a hostage to fortune. I, of all people! Now I remember why I was so reluctant to do this.

On the fifth day a woman who isn't a nurse or doctor comes to my bedside with some paperwork and says rather briskly: 'You do realize we need this bed, don't you? You can't stay here.'

'Of course. Sorry.'

We put my things into a bag and go down to the nursery.

'Oh, you'll be able to come back and get him quite soon,' says the doctor on duty.

'Er . . .'

'Come back . . .?'

'Fine,' says Peter. 'When?'

'Ooh, shouldn't be longer than a week.'

'Right. So . . .'

'We have to go home without him.'

Peter is being even nicer to me than usual, and watches me constantly, as if expecting me to be traumatized. But since I have never been at home with a baby in the first place, it doesn't feel that bad – just weird. Have I had a baby? The cards say I have. Peter makes supper and we read them all.

'And hey, what's this?'

'Chocolate cake!'

The card says: *Love from Patrick & Sheila. There are times when only chocolate cake will do.*

They're right. We have two pieces each and go to bed in our new life, a limbo between being parents and not being parents. Then we get up and go to the hospital and sit by the incubator with the other regulars, all with our various offerings, like worshippers at a very high-tech shrine. When one of the others has extra family in, we all give them our chairs. The room is small, yet when a cot alarm goes off, the space expands to accommodate an entire trauma team, which descends in moments and then vanishes again.

After a few days of this, one of the consultants says: 'Lawrence is nearly ready to go home.'

'Hooray! When?'

'All you have to do is establish feeding, and when he's put on enough weight . . .'

'How much is enough?'

'Ooh, don't worry: it shouldn't be a problem.'

We should know by now that that is doctor talk for *difficult, very difficult, excessively difficult* or *likely to cause you to scream.*

We are shown into a tiny room with a bed, cupboard and TV, next to the nurses' coffee room. The furniture is in that orangey sort of wood.

'Early Seventies Dolls' House, would you say?'

'Definitely style-free. And look: the window's sealed shut.'

I have sunk from my prime position on the fifth floor to a basement cell. At the top of the window we can see feet.

'Go and ask them for a better room.'

'A suite?'

'Yeah. With minibar.'

'What are we supposed to do?'

We are supposed to sleep – hah – on the narrow single bed, then every two to four hours or so, they'll bang on the door and get me up to feed Lawrence. Then, when they've weighed him and he's heavy enough, we can take him home.

After the third bang on the door and no sleep, Peter says: 'This is like being in prison.'

'Yeah, but you're not the one who's just had a midwife grab your tit.'

'What?!'

'That weird one with the Max Bygraves wig. She grabbed me!'

'Bloody hell.'

'I don't think it was foreplay. She was supposedly showing me how to feed.'

'Can we just hurry up and get out of here?'

'All right! You're not the one on trial with the weighing.'

'I'm with you all the way, you know that.'

'Yeah, but – Peter?'

'Zzzzzzzzzzzzzzzzzz.'

The feeding is hard enough, but the weighing is horrendous.

'How much? How much?'

'Three grams.'

'Shit . . .'

Peter feeds me up with takeaways and shortbread biscuits, but after two nights I feel as though I've been there all my life. Tilly and Claudia, my two oldest friends, arrive together and behave as though this is completely normal. Peter goes into the corridor so we can sit together on the tiny bed.

'I've never been a student,' I say. 'Is it very like this?'

'Oh, yeah,' says Claudia, 'put up a Che Guevara poster and – you're not writing any essays, are you? That's it: you're there.'

By the end of the third day Lawrence is still refusing to put on weight.

'This is hopeless. We're never going to be able to take him home. What shall we do?!'

'I dunno. Are we eligible for parole?'

That evening one of the consultants sits us down and says: 'Look. What I think you should do is—'

'Oh, my God! What?'

'Go out to dinner.'

'What?'

'There's a very nice place just up there. Go on. You need a treat.'

'Go *out*?! What if he wakes up?'

'Don't worry. Give yourself a couple of hours. He'll be fine.'

'You mean we can just go?'

'Go on! I'm prescribing it!'

We go and have green curry and beers.

The next day they weigh Lawrence and say: 'Yup, he's fine. You can take him home.'

'What, really?'

'Are you sure?'

Peter goes to get the car.

'Shit!'

'What?!'

'It's only got two doors.'

'What d'you mean? Of course it – Ah . . .'

To twist round and get this fragile, breakable heirloom into the new baby seat takes forty minutes. Also, the street looks different. It's NOISY and DIRTY and full of DANGER, like CARS and LORRIES and people going to and from A&E who might be PSYCHOS. Peter holds him tightly and looks both ways before even crossing the pavement, like a Secret Service man. Then we get in and drive home, at four miles an hour.

It's exciting to have Lawrence in our own domain at last. But after a few days he starts to cry. A lot. More and more. He starts to feed, then snaps off, crying. He doesn't seem hungry. Hopeless as I am, I can already tell that this is not usual. It goes on and on. Peter and I talk about it, stare at him, stare at him again, and conclude that we have no idea what's going on.

We try the dummy. As well as producing a pleasingly affronted expression on the faces of people who disapprove, it gives us some peace and quiet. *You are stifling the natural cry of your baby*, says a book I pick up in a shop somewhere. Isn't that the *point*? As my dad used to say, '*Can't you go and express yourself somewhere else?*' Anyhow, Lawrence is expressing himself all right. And nothing, but nothing, gives him relief.

'Maybe we should take him to the health visitor.'

'Oh no! She'll say it's my fault.'

So we continue to pace round him, pick him up, put him down and stare pointlessly.

After three days of this I pluck up courage and go. Carol is not how I imagined a health visitor would be. She sounds like an academic, but much humbler, with an almost inaudible voice – quite a challenge when dispensing vital information about things like vaccines.

'So, I'll just pop him on the scale, shall I?' She is being very gentle. Her voice, if that is possible, is even quieter than usual. Lawrence is put in the big white scoop, like an ingredient for some hideous recipe. But Carol is not witch-like. She breaks the news in a whisper.

'Ah.'

'What? *What?!*'

'He hasn't put on very much weight.'

'How much?'

'Well, only a few grams.'

'In a WEEK?'

'Yes . . . Don't worry. He's fine.'

'Oh my God . . .'

I sink into a chair. I Have Failed To Nourish My Child. He is crying because he is HUNGRY. That's why he kept snapping off the nipple. He's hungry, and it is my fault. I am STARVING him to DEATH. Well, that makes perfect sense, doesn't it? I would starve my child. I knew I should never have taken this on. '*But you don't like children,*' someone said when I was pregnant. Even when I *say* I like them, I don't really. I harm them. I am a Bad Person. I don't deserve this baby.

Carol says: 'It might be a good idea, if you don't object' – her voice drops even further – 'to give him a bottle of formula.' A *BOTTLE*? In *Islington*? I can see a Bateman cartoon: *The Health Visitor Who Suggested a Bottle*. Any minute now the Parenting Police will swarm in and take us both away. Relief sweeps over me. *There is help for people like you.* And failure: I *am* redundant – so soon. 'You don't have to stop breastfeeding, unless you want to. He can have both.'

'And Peter can feed him as well!'

She also tells me that she, her sister and her mother all had the same problem. All my life I've overeaten, except for now. Now, when I finally *need* to eat, I can't. Ever since I came home from hospital without him, I've had no appetite. No wonder there's no milk. What a time to diet! If it weren't so tragic it would be funny. Carol is so quiet now I can't hear her. Oh, she's not talking: she's *listening*.

'Why don't you put him on now, for a bit, while we talk?'

I talk for an hour. Feeding him was something *I* could do. No one else. And now I can't even do that. But just saying it makes me feel better. She listens for an hour. At the end of it, I am lighter in every respect.

But this is the Beginning of the End. I've lost my exclusive contract. I'm not indispensable, and Lawrence is on his way to independence. First stop: SMA, then crossing the road by himself. Soon: college. I feel as though I'm giving him his freedom, not least by not starving him any more. *I do so find it helps, don't you, to start life on a full stomach?*

I go to Boots, to buy the dreaded tin. Back home, I check my two books on breastfeeding.

'*Some women worry about not having enough milk. Relax: this cannot happen!*'

We carry on with breast and bottle. Peter gets to do his bit and we both start to feel useful. But another few days on, it starts to hurt. A LOT. Each suck is suddenly like having my nipple shut in a serrated metal vice – if I knew what that was like, which thank God I don't, but I imagine it feels very like this. I know if you get only the nipple in and not the surrounding area it hurts, but he *has* got the surrounding area. He has, he has, he HAS! On the other hand, what else can I do? The books don't give me another strategy. I take him off and put him back on, pointlessly. Every time he goes back on, it feels like someone shutting my nipple in a door. I look down, just to check whether the hospital has given me a baby with metal teeth.

Peter tiptoes round me like a man nostalgic for the good old days of PMT.

'Is it . . .?'

'It *HURTS*!' I scream. My teeth are actually gritted.

What was he going to ask me? How many breastfeeding women it takes to change a lightbulb? *Just smash the bulb over my head: it has to feel better than this.*

I take Lawrence off again, and put him back on. He seems to be latched on correctly, so why the fuck is it still *hurting so much*? It's excruciating, and there's *no way out*.

Peter says: 'D'you want me to give him a bottle?'

'NO, BECAUSE IF I *DON'T* FEED HIM, MY BREASTS FILL UP AND GO ALL HARD AGAIN!' I can't win. I know because our friend Vida invited us for supper and from 6 p.m. he slept.

'Great!' we said. 'We can eat, drink and talk for six hours.'

But that was six hours he didn't feed, obviously, and when I got up from the table my tits had solidified, like bricks. My left arm felt weird, and when I tried to move it, I couldn't. *Is she serious?* Yes, my left side had seized up completely. So there you have it; you can go from only managing ten millilitres an hour to having so much it fills up your arm.

I need something to bite on: my mother. She is staying and ventures an opinion.

'You're expecting it to hurt. If you tense up and *expect* it to hurt, it will.'

Not tensing is her answer to everything. *All you have to do is the Natural Childbirth breathing.* Pain in childbirth – you were tensing. Pain at the doctor – injections, smear tests, having your leg off – you weren't doing the breathing. There is no such thing as pain, in the objective, empirical sense. Run over? It wouldn't have hurt if you'd been doing the breathing. Rwanda? You haven't had your head cut off with a machete: you just weren't doing the breathing. I put Lawrence back on again, and wince.

'No, no, look: like this.' She breathes v-e-r-y s-l-o-w-l-y. 'You're not doing it!' She shrugs and walks off.

Shortly afterwards, when I am hoping for death as a merciful release, a nice man who works for Peter comes round with a present for Lawrence. He takes in the expression on my face – so unlike the one on the posters, and says: 'We had some trouble with this, too. Would you like the number of our breastfeeding counsellor?'

I can no longer speak, so Peter says: 'Yes, please.'

The breastfeeding counsellor is from the NCT. She comes round, takes one look at me and says: 'Oh yes, there they are.'

'There what are?'

'White patches. Go to the doctor, get her to look in Lawrence's mouth and they'll probably be there too.'

'What will? What is it?'

'No wonder you were sore. You've both got thrush.'

And suddenly I don't care about the pain any more, because this proves I'm not stupid or mad. We get some ointment and the pain starts to go away. And I know that not to have sore tits is all I will ever ask for in life, ever.

5 Chain Gang

After four weeks, Peter goes back to work.

'Bye, Lawrence! Bye, darling! Have a good day!'

Oh, God . . .

'You too! See you at – *oh no* – suppertime.'

Don't go! Please, please don't go! I don't know what to do! It's all been a mistake! Please, oh please!

I've been left alone in the house with a *baby*. Me. Wasn't it just a short while ago I left a toothbrush at Peter's flat for the first time, and thought, *hey this isn't too bad* . . . Then we moved in together, didn't we . . . and got married – uh-oh, that was quite grown-up – and then I let go of my flat . . . that was a *really* big deal . . . and then we bought this place, which was even *more* scary. And now—

Omigod, omigod, omigod. I got carried away, that's what I did. I keep hearing my friend Alison's answerphone message from when we first told her our news.

'*I bet you're thinking: I've been and gone and done it now . . .*'

It was the truest thing anyone said to me that whole nine months.

I can feel the panic rising in my throat, like sick.

There's a person, who I don't really know, in my house. And he's completely dependent on me.

What do I DO? When Peter was here we could be confused together. But on my own ... It's like one of those dreams where you're in a play and don't know the lines. There's plenty of advice on the shelves about supporting his head, or dipping your elbow in the water to check the temperature of a bath. But now, right now, alone in this room, what do I do? It's slightly embarrassing. I mean, I don't want to ignore him. And yet I don't know what to say. This feeling reminds me of – God, it's a blind date.

I've made a mistake. It's like thinking I could perform at Wembley Arena when I've never even sung in public. Or go on the West End stage. Or fly. What ever possessed me to think I – I, of all people – could do this? Just because I went into Marks & Spencer's a few times and wept over the tiny socks – I was allowed to be an actual *mother*? Because I was interested, because I was curious – does that make me *qualified*? I'm interested in film-making; that doesn't make me Ingmar Bloody Bergman. The sheer chutzpah, the affrontery of it, makes me gasp. I remember an old saying, *Beware of what you want: you may get it.* First, I wanted my independence and my father died. Now *this*. I feel like a mortal in one of those awful Greek myths who makes the wrong wish. We all know about Midas, but I'm thinking of Eos, the Dawn, who was tricked into asking Zeus for a wish. She asked that her husband should never die.

'*Is that your only wish?*' said Zeus, and she said. '*Yes.*'

The husband was young and beautiful for a few years, then started to get older – and older.

'*What's happening?*' she cried. '*You promised he would never die!*' And Zeus said: '*You didn't ask that he should remain forever young.*'

Eventually he was a tiny, shrivelled thing, skittering down the palace corridors like a grasshopper.

I've got to *CALM THE FUCK DOWN*.

I sit on the sofa, clutching this – stranger. Maybe I should go to the lavatory. I always feel calm in there. No, I'd have to put him down. My whole body is so tensed, I'm barely sitting on the sofa at all. My arse is so high I'm nearer the ceiling.

Maybe I'll wait. Only eight hours till Peter gets home.

I won't ignore him. I may be a shit mother but I do have some manners.

'Well! Here we are! I'm your mummy.'

This is pathetic. One thing at a time, come on, do something! People do this – thick people! I plump the cushions round us.

'Why don't we have a video?' We've got loads. I have a look through some of the things we've taped over the months and indeed years. *Waco: the Rise and Fall of David Koresh* . . . *Myra Hindley, Portrait of a Killer* . . . *The Unabomber.* Or there are always the six episodes of *Perpetual Motion: Great Transport Designs that Refused to Die, Classic Cars, Classic Trains* and *Classic Planes.* Peter's keeping all of them on the grounds that in a couple of years Lawrence will talk of little else. Well, while I've still got control of the remote: Hmm . . . *Dr Strangelove* – not quite. *The Fly* . . . *Bonnie and Clyde* . . . *La Reine Margot* – featuring the Technicolor massacre of the Protestants in sixteenth-century France. *Homicide* . . . *Love Child* – what was that? Oh, yes: unmarried women in the Sixties whose babies were taken away from them.

Hey, I could read a book! I've been meaning to do that since I left school. I take Lawrence over to the bookshelves. A friend's given me a book of stories about Motherhood, inscribed: *Just the right length to read between feeds!* But I can't face a load of essays where people stare into their baby's cot and go all *intense.* Actually, books are too sort of – wordy. Maybe I'll read one when I get in the swing of it more. When he starts crawling; I'll read then. Or when he learns to walk.

'I know! Let's put on the TV.' Daytime TV's allowed if you've just had a baby, right? *The Time, The Place* is starting, but even that seems a bit challenging.

Noon. I need to wee. I put him down and get up. He sort of warbles. I sit down again and pick him up. What shall I do? We once gave a mobile to a friend who'd just had a baby. She sent us a photo of him in his cot, gazing up at it. On the back of it she'd written: *Thank you – I have now been to the lavatory for the first time in eight weeks.* At the time I thought: *How totally ridiculous! Why doesn't she just GO?* But that was before I discovered how hard it is to leave the room.

I try wedging him in with the cushions. He whimpers. I pick him up, then try to put him back down again, v-e-r-y s-l-o-w-l-y so he won't notice. I take a step or two. He cries. He doesn't want me to go. I try again. As with trying to walk past spiders, I take small steps backwards and forwards for what seems hours before giving up in defeat. He cries. I pick him up and sit down with him again. The loo is only on the landing. Look! I can see it, twelve stairs away. I sit down again. I don't need to go *that* badly. I'm sure I can wait until Peter comes home; it's only another six hours.

With Lawrence on my chest facing me, the way he sometimes sleeps at night, we both fall asleep. The feeling of drifting away is like a fantastic drug.

I wake up with a terrible ache in my bladder, and an idea. I could bring him with me! We go upstairs together, and he lies on the carpeted landing two feet away from me, while I pee.

'Wow! That was wonderful!'

We go back to the sofa again. I'm hungry, but the kitchen is downstairs. Come to think of it, this isn't a good house to have a baby in. Everything is on another floor. Why didn't we just move to a lighthouse? I pick him up, and go gingerly down the horribly steep staircase, at about one step a minute. It has definitely got steeper since we moved in. Now what? There's a loaf of bread on the counter, but unsliced. I'll need two hands to cut it.

Like the great explorers sailing through unchartered waters in the quest for El Dorado, I'm driven forward by the thought of Toast. Eventually, after about four false starts, I hold Lawrence very tightly against me with one arm, and use that hand to steady the bread while I cut it with the other.

'Better have two slices,' I tell him. 'Don't know when we'll be able to make it back, do we?' I have butter and Marmite on it. It is the best meal I have ever had.

After a week of this, I start to feel – as Withnail put it – *unusual*.

Shelley, my neighbour opposite, has also had a baby. She rings me and says: 'Shall we push our prams down to the swings?' To my fevered brain it sounds like: *'Shall we cross the Arctic Circle in white stilettos and no tights?'* But it's only September, and still sunny out there. The swings are in the little square at the end of the road. There are roses. I've had a lot of flowers in bunches recently; it would be amazing to see some growing in the ground.

We do even have a pram, from a friend of Peter's. It's a nice turquoise colour, but very *low*. I'm not tall, and I have to bend down to reach the handle. Semi-crouched, like a cartoon of a burglar, I follow Shelley down to the square. The colour of the flowers nearly sends my retinas into spasm.

YELLOW!

RED!

PINK!

Conversation is beyond me; I sink onto a bench and stare. She doesn't say much either. But a thrilling new vista has opened up. We walk home in triumph.

'Hello, sweetness. How was your day?'

'I went to the square! With Shelley! It was brilliant!'

'The square—'

'At the end of the road!'

'That's – wonderful.'

'Yeah! We just – took the prams and went! It was great!'

'Well done!'

Looking back on it, I probably should have got out more.

That evening, I tell Peter about my adventures in the next postcode, while he gives Lawrence his SMA. Having forgotten to heat the first bottle, we've simply carried on with it at room temperature – breaking another of these so-called 'rules'.

'And now . . .' he says, eyes gleaming, 'I have a present for you.'

'For me?!'

'Well, kind of.'

He pours me a glass of wine and opens a flat cardboard box. Inside is a baby chair, made of cloth stretched over a wire frame, like a 'V' on its side.

'I've heard of these!'

'This,' he says, 'will give you your arms back. Lawrence, you are about to go in the Bouncy Chair!'

'Not – the *Bouncy Chair*?'

'Yes, the Bouncy Chair!'

It looks a bit as though, when we let go, it might catapult him across the room. We ease him in, do up the little seat belt, and slowly, ever so slowly, let go. The seat wobbles slightly, as it's meant to, and Lawrence seems – if not ecstatic, at least not to mind. Peter raises his glass.

'We've had a baby!'

And I think: *OK. We've got everything we need. Please don't ever leave the house again.*

6 Baby à la Carte

On a noticeboard somewhere, I see an appeal for babies to help with research in the Eye Department of London University. I go along several times.

'What's it for?' says Peter.

'I dunno. They have chocolate biscuits. And people to talk to.'

'Sounds good. Can you spin it out?'

'Not too much. I have to pace myself.'

And indeed, the sheer thrill of putting Lawrence in the car and meeting other adult humans is enough to last me all week. What with that and going out for nappies, life is a whirl.

A friend brings round a sterilizer.

'You'll be needing this,' she says. Peter and I look at each other.

'That's lovely!' he says. 'Thank you so much!'

After she's gone, we put it away in a cupboard. One of the benefits of being stuck in the Neonatal Unit for two weeks was the opportunity to bother the staff with questions.

'What about sterilizing?' was one. 'Do we need to do that?' Along with his job of fetching me coffee and takeaways, Peter sees his role as editing the parental task load. He loves to seek out and eliminate bits of unnecessary procedure.

The nurse says: 'Actually, no. In fact, we don't really recommend sterilizing.'

'You *don't*?! Great!'

'What people don't realize is, you still have to wash the things in any case. But because they're sterilizing, they often don't wash them properly. Have you got a dishwasher?' We got one as a wedding present! 'Well, our micro-biologist says just use that. Sixty degrees and you'll be fine.'

'Way-hey!' says Peter. 'No sterilizing!'

It's the parental equivalent of being told you never have to shave your legs. We try to share the good news, but when we mention it to one or two friends, they clearly think we've gone mad. But that's fine. We don't mind the sterilizer in the cupboard. Everyone's giving us their used baby gear, and it's brilliant.

'The house is turning into a jumble sale,' says Peter.

'I know! Isn't it great?!'

So far we have a cot and cot bedding from Marie, a

great pile of clothes from Claudia, a sling from Vicki, the pram from Sam – sounds like a Dr Seuss story – and a burgeoning store of smart winter coats and other worn-once chic stuff from mother of triplets Judith. My mum has got a second-hand cot for £20 to use when we come to her place, and a second-hand playpen (£10) 'for the crawling stage – or you'll have to watch him every minute.' Peter has found a pushchair – for six months onwards – in a skip. There is, however, one item I do need to buy.

I go back to John Lewis – on my own with Lawrence – and buy myself a baby bag: a soft, black Fiorelli briefcase. It is made of that shinyish material, with a zip you can pull easily with one hand, a shoulder strap and a pocket on the outside for wipes. It does not have bunnies on it. Afterwards, I go for lunch and eat soup over Lawrence's head; he is sleeping so nicely in the sling, and also if I take him out, I can't always quite remember how to retie it. Even going to the loo is possible without unloading; I just lift him up slightly like a detachable beer gut. When I come back home and take him off, I feel cold and a bit naked.

After this I am ambitious for new horizons. Peter has passes to the Motor Show, so Lawrence can get his first view of the new TVRs, and we can experience the hell that is taking a pushchair on the tube. But it isn't hell at all – it's fine! All you have to do is make sure you have a man with you at all times, to carry the whole lot up and down the stairs.

Olympia is bristling with ultra-blokes, most with cameras. We sit down for lunch on the Honda stand, and Lawrence immediately wakes up and cries.

'Hungry,' says Peter, perceptively.

I look round for a suitable place. I've seen the loos already, and they're cold and concrete with no chairs. It'd be like breastfeeding in an underpass.

'Come on,' says Peter, 'it'll be fine.'

'But . . .' Then Lawrence ups the volume, and I get my next taste of that thing I thought only Proper Mothers had: instinct. I stick him on, and we continue to chat about this year's models. No one from Honda tells me to put them away, or that in Japan, a woman doing this in public brings shame on her ancestors. A man shares our table. He has a notebook, a tape recorder and a huge backpack containing – a toddler. My God: we're not unique! As we walk round, people on various stands – male and female – admire Lawrence and stop us to talk.

'Ah, makes me miss my little boy,' says a bloke from BMW.

'Ooh, can I hold him? Here, you go and get yourselves a cup of tea,' says a woman from Rolls-Royce. While

Lawrence is passed round, Peter and I get in and out of the new TVR Cerbera, the new Ford Ka and the new Alfa 156 with concealed rear-door handles.

'Hey, look at this!'

'You think it's only got two doors, but it's actually got four.'

'It doesn't *look* child-friendly—'

'But it is!'

We put our names down for one, and go home thrilled.

Then one morning, a funny thing happens. It's been an average night. We got up about three times; I barked at Peter's boss when he woke me by ringing at 10 p.m. Anyhow, I pick Lawrence up, shuffle downstairs to the kettle, and feel something is different. Not the room: it's still littered with the same mess as the night before. When I look at him, there's a new feeling, quite strong. It isn't like the pain I felt in hospital, when that nurse wouldn't take him out of the incubator, and it's not like the guilt when he didn't put on weight. All the other feelings I've felt so far – pride, triumph, outrage, contentedness – have had to break through an overweening layer of fear: fear that something bad is about to happen all the time, and fear that I have Made the Wrong Choice. But today, a normal day with nothing new to look forward to, no prospect of novelty – the fear has subsided a little. I am experiencing a sensation that *is* new. Yet it's also strangely familiar. Is it merely the absence of fear? No, something more. Suddenly it clicks.

I'M IN LOVE! WHOOPEE! This is AMAZING. Ooooooh. Wowwwww! I wonder if anyone else knows about this? I must tell them. I must tell everyone. I must spread the Good News, so that all personkind can worship this heavenly – uh-oh. OK, I get it now. Stand down the angels and shepherds. Cancel the star in the east.

'Hey, husband!'

'What?'

'I think I've just bonded.'

'There, you see? I told you not to worry.'

'No, no: you don't understand. I think I'm in love.'

'What about me?'

'You've served your purpose. Tell you what, though.'

'What?'

'You've got *lovely* DNA.'

It has taken me twelve and a half weeks. Can't find that in the books either. Can't find the bit that says: '*You may bond quickly, like superglue, or you may be the slow-acting kind, where the two parts must be held together for some time until they stick.*'

Weirdly, at around the same time, I am beginning to

think it might be nice, now and then, to have a break. I am clear that I love this baby I've had for nearly four months, but I'm also rather missing my Self. And the space that used to be around me when I was detached. I wonder if I could – no, I can't. I feel guilty at even having the thought.

Nick comes round for supper. He is in his sixties, a journalist and grandfather. We have tremendous confidence in him. He can write you 1,000 words on anything and sound like an expert. And just having an older person in the house, we discover, can be immensely reassuring.

When he arrives, I am cooking – distractedly – while Peter tries to get Lawrence to go to sleep. The magic he can work, with his forwards-and-backwards swaying, is totally absent tonight. Why *do* babies go to sleep sometimes when you want them to, then suddenly not? Why do they feed for so long? Is there a pipe going through them, leading to ten other babies all having a drink at the same time? We pace around, pondering these pointless questions, while Lawrence grizzles. Suddenly Nick looks up and says, 'D'you want a hand?'

He puts him up against his shoulder, as Peter has just done, sits down and says, 'Now, stop bothering your parents and go to sleep, will you? There's a good chap.' Then he gets out a copy of the *Financial Times*.

Lawrence is asleep within seconds. In the kitchen, Peter and I lose concentration on the dinner as we marvel at this mystical event. Is it the upright position? Well, yes, but we did that and it didn't work. Is it the deep voice? Possibly: babies are supposed not to like shrieks. But then, Peter's voice is hardly Julian Clary-ish, and I sound like Michael Buerk. Also, there is no one bouncing up and down, jiggling him – *that* helps. But maybe Lawrence is just at that moment ready to drop off. There is the x-factor, certainly: the mysterious alignment of the planets that causes children suddenly to do what you want. There is one more thing, though: more to do with what Nick isn't, than what he is. He isn't Lawrence's parent, and as such has no huge investment in his going to sleep. He doesn't – ultimately – *care*. And that's where he has the edge.

This proves that *anyone* can be parental, not just a mother and clearly not just women. Often *not* women: I am proof of that. You can be a man, and not related to the infant at all.

A vision forms in my head ... of me, Peter and perhaps a third person – to Help.

But it's a crazy idea, and anyhow, we don't know anyone. I'm not ready to go back to work, and anyhow the whole idea is – when you really think about it – too terrifying. Like many people nowadays, we have family either too spread out geographically, or not in a position to help. And in any case, there aren't enough of them. The 'extended family group' ideal my mother waxes on about is hard to assemble when all you've got is a sister each, both with full-time jobs, sixty miles apart. Anyhow, they need their own time. One has finished her family and the other hasn't begun. They're doing other things with their lives. Besides, there is a downside to family – well, mine anyway: they have an opinion about *everything*. A person we pay could give advice but we needn't have to listen. We'd be in charge!

'We could get an au pair,' says Peter. 'I could show her around . . .'

'Good luck to you,' I say. 'Sad old git.'

Anyhow, I want someone who knows more than me, not less. But who? We ask Claudia.

'I got Bobbie from a magazine,' she says. 'Been with us for three years.'

'Hmmm.' But she's confident and relaxed.

'I used an agency,' says Barbara. 'But they sent someone with an awful boyfriend who banged on the door at night.'

'Hadn't they checked?'

'They said, "*If we'd told you, you might not have given her the job.*" '

'!'

92

'Exactly.'

'Advertise in *The Lady*,' says Jane. 'That's what all my friends do.'

'Much too scary. And I'd have to interview people.'

'I don't mind interviewing,' says Peter, 'but I still want a personal recommendation.'

To see what it feels like, we ask my friend Alison to babysit. She has two boys at primary school *and* works, *and* is learning to drive, *and* is currently repainting her flat. She's like a throwback to an earlier generation, the sort you could imagine welding Spitfires in a hairnet.

'D'you think you could cope with Lawrence while we go to the cinema?' we ask her.

'Don't be silly. I thought you'd never ask!'

She puts him in his car seat on the table, where her boys gaze at him in wonderment.

'Get on with your homework!' she says.

'Isn't she *amazing*?' we say, as we drive away.

Discovering we can cope with having a few hours to ourselves, we start asking people we know if they have any great nannies they don't need any more.

But the nannies of people we know – if we could afford them, which we can't – are all fully employed, working for people we know. There is no equivalent of 'Shea' – Pat O'Shea – who looked after my sister and me. Shea is great with children despite having had none of her own. Come to think of it, she'd had no previous experience at all before coming to us, but those were less anxious times. She had sound instincts about kids and and her techniques always got results. When I locked myself in the bathroom at three, she offered me a chocolate bar which helped me remember how to work the bolt. And when I flushed her gold watch down the lavatory, she didn't even shout at me. Hell, the woman could write a book on kids – ten books. She's perfect! There is one little problem, though; she is now seventy-seven.

Another month goes by. Wherever we go, we ask for recommendations, but the horizon is bare. I begin to resign myself to a lifetime at home. My career – so important to me, so long fought for – will wither away. Eventually I'll be someone who *used to write once*, the glory days of pop star interviews and Fleet Street gossip a speck on the viewfinder of Time ... Shit! Look what's happening to my style! I've already gone stale.

A couple of weeks later I bring Lawrence back to Carol, the quiet-voiced health visitor. She puts him in the scales, congratulates me on his weight gain, and lays him down to measure his length. Then she says, out of nowhere:

'Do you want a childminder? Only I know a really good one, and she's got a space.'

'God! Are you telepathic as well?!'

'She almost never gets spaces – only really when people move away. And someone has. Here's her number, if you want to give her a ring.'

This is typical; the moment you give up on something, along it comes. I take the number back to Peter, holding it carefully in case it explodes in my bag.

7 I Give My Baby Away

My mother wags a middle-class finger: 'Childminder? She'll put him in front of the TV all day, and *smoke*.'

Maureen lives on a respectable council estate of houses with little gardens, gradually going private. No one has written *Kelly is a Slag* on any of the walls. No children try to sell us crack or offer to mind our car for a pound. A gate opens into a small yard full of trikes and pedal cars. The house is warm and spotless. In the kitchen, two little boys, aged two at a guess, are playing with a toy garage. We stand there, and I know Peter's thinking the same as me: *I hope she doesn't ask us anything too difficult.* Luckily, Maureen knows the questions as well as the answers; without actually saying, *'You don't know what you're doing, do you?'* she succeeds in imparting the information. This is good because we have no idea what we're supposed to ask.

She speaks in soft, measured tones. As someone who babbles, and too loudly, I've always been fascinated by people who can command attention by saying relatively little, and without barking. Where children are involved, it's really impressive.

The whole atmosphere is cosy, safe and deeply restful – like sinking into a bath. The two boys vroom their cars up and down the gleaming kitchen floor, and we notice another baby of Lawrence's age, sleeping in a pram. How could anyone look after this lot and be so *calm*? How could anyone get their house that *clean*? Maybe she'll spoil it all by turning out to be insufferably smug. She insists we follow up at least two of her references. She opens a folder full of letters, and gives us a few to read. While we talk, she asks to hold Lawrence, which she does with great tenderness yet a marked lack of fuss. She's older than me, and far wiser – which at this stage wouldn't be difficult. She's only forty-two to my thirty-seven. But her own sons are nearly grown-up. She is, in terms of experience, another generation.

We say goodbye, put Lawrence back in the pram and walk home.

'Well!' said Peter. 'I don't know what Lawrence thought, but I'd *love* to stay there all day and play with the toy garage.'

'We can't,' I said.

'I know . . . Pity.'

'No, I mean I can't do it.'

'What?! I thought you really liked her. Blimey, have I misread the situation completely?'

'It just seems so cruel.'

'What? I thought you wanted a break.'

'I do, but it's inhumane – what were we *thinking* of? We can't give him away.'

'We're not Giving Him Away: you're having a break. You deserve a few hours to yourself.'

'I can't.'

'Well, what about work? You want to go back to writing at some point, don't you? It'll enable you to do that.'

'Yeah, I miss my work. No, I don't: I miss my freedom. Oh, God, that's *really* bad.'

'No it isn't.'

'I love him! But I'd love a break, too. It's hard, doing this all day and night. But that's because I'm not a Proper Mother. Proper Mothers can do it. Proper Mothers don't give their children away.'

'You *are* a Proper Mother. You're not Giving Him Away.'

Poor Peter. As my boyfriend he was spared the '*I'm Fat*'/'*No you're not*' conversation, only to end up with *this*.

'Look it's your decision. Whatever you want is fine with me.' Oh, cheers. That's the trouble with these men

98

who let you make your own decisions; you can't blame them when things go wrong.

'I know!' he says that evening. 'Let's ring the references. With any luck they'll tell us that she beats them and feeds them on nothing but Pop Tarts, and the decision will be made for us.'

On the list there are two architects, parents of the baby asleep in the pram, and two GPs – the parents of one of the boys playing with the garage. The other one's parents are teachers.

'Well, we've found the catch,' says Peter. 'She won't take us unless we both do exactly the same job.'

None of them has anything bad to say. We ring the woman who's moved to Shropshire, who's created the empty place. 'My only regret about leaving London,' she says, 'is losing Maureen.'

'What do *you* want?' Peter asks me.

People who like looking after children all day long – even their own – are one kind of person. People who prefer to be at work for a full day are another kind. And what do I want? Neither. And both. Too much time at home with the baby, and I'll go mad. I'm already feeling quite weird from not going out enough. However, not enough time with him and I'll go mad there as well. Considering most people don't get their first choice, whatever it is, I'm very lucky. I can write part of the time, and not write part of the time, which is what I've always done anyway. Except that now I have an actual reason for not working that hard. Why didn't I do this before? If I'd saved all that shirking time I could have had five children by now.

'Why don't we give it a try?' says Peter reasonably. 'If we don't like it – if you're not happy – we'll stop. OK?'

Does he deliberately wait for me to wear myself out before invariably coming up with a solution, or does he just coincidentally always think of it just as I grind to a halt?

'Yeah. I'm tired,' I say. 'Pour me a drink, will you?'

Meanwhile we're working up to the First Solids, an event which in retrospect occupies an unjustifiably prominent position in the infant CV. Lawrence eats his mashed banana, looking at us as if to say, 'So?'

The baby rice is also an anticlimax, in that he eats it. By Boxing Day we're blasé enough to give him mashed potato and gravy, which he pukes up. I sing '*Night and Day*', and he laughs – one of the kinder reactions I've had to my singing. On the third day of the new year he grasps his bottle.

'He's a genius!'

'Look at those opposable thumbs.'

We visit two-year-old Jack, who generously offers Lawrence use of his classic pedal Mercedes.

'Did anyone ever tell you,' says Jack's mother Rose, 'how soon they start to be a source of Light Entertainment?'

'No, I thought you had to wait till they were at least thirty-five.'

She stirs her casserole. 'It's a bit like having Sky.'

On 15 January I wake at 5.10 a.m., convinced I'm going to be struck down by lightning for consorting with a childminder. We both take Lawrence along for his first half-day, and Maureen asks us to take a picture of them together, which we still have: she's crouching in the yard with him on her knee, looking up at us as if to say: *'It's OK, you're not bad parents. He'll be Fine,'* and he's in his blue and white matching suit and hat, gazing off to the side as if to say, *'I AM fine. Go on, shove off.'*

'Are you sure it's OK?'

'He'll be fine.'

'Look, Lawrence: a Wendy house.'

'Actually, we're not allowed to call it that,' says Maureen. 'The Council says it's sexist.'

'What do you have to call it, then?'

'We have to say Play House.'

We say goodbye, and leave, feeling extremely brave.

'Wendy house! Wendy house!'

'Come on,' says Peter. 'You're disturbing the neighbours.'

As we walk down the road, he squeezes my arm and we look at each other. Another milestone! He goes to work, and I get a bus to Oxford Street – not to buy anything, but just to try it 'naked'.

Lawrence settles into his routine. At 9 a.m. he goes to Maureen's, and I wander around town, heady with the excitement of it all, and amazed that it can feel so normal. At 1 p.m. I collect him. As she likes to give all the children lunch before going to the One O'Clock Club, I have to bring some jars or a packet which she can make up. I bring some organic jars to start with, then, when she keeps running out because I never bring enough, some boxes of dried baby food, of dubious constitution. It looks like sawdust, and is probably less organic than what we put in the car. The power trip, though, is quite thrilling. Is it really up to *me*?

Whatever I do, however bumbling and disorganized I am, she gives the impression I'm doing fine. Coming from a family in which you're constantly told how to do even the most basic things, I find this exhilarating. In my early twenties I lived for a while in Dubai. My mother was deeply concerned that I'd have to drive on the other side of the road, and was sure there must be a separate manual which I'd have to read first. The feeling, when I turned the key and set off perfectly well on the right, made me wonder whether I'd been brought up just to be a *teensy bit too cautious*. The remarkable thing about talented people, I realize, is that even when they're far better than you are at something, they empower you to feel you're brilliant too. Mr Silverstone had that quality: saying, '*Well done!*' to someone after an elective C-section almost certainly isn't in the NHS Guidelines; nor is addressing the patient as '*Commander*' as he did on his ward round. Maureen makes me feel – *competent*. Life really could run smoothly after all. I could gradually restart work. Peter and I could get a babysitter and go to the cinema. Anything's possible! I feel a stab of guilt, then more guilt because by my reckoning, I don't feel guilty *enough*.

We soon solve *that* problem. We've just discovered another thing that isn't in the books, which is that whichever stage you're anticipating your child is about to move on to, they're guaranteed to get there first. Today, for example, we are about to find out that Lawrence is now able to turn over by himself. It's Friday, and Peter has left work early so we can beat the rush-hour traffic to my mother's. We lie Lawrence on the sofa, move away to put various things in bags, and *BLAM*! He is lying on the carpet. He is not visibly injured, but crying hard.

'Right!' says Peter. 'A&E. Quickly!'

'Are you sure?'

'What do you mean, are you sure?'

I'm thinking about having to wait around for hours among those coughing, twitching people who live in A&E. I'm feeling guilty, but not for the same reason as he is. He's thinking, Our Child Could Be Hurt, and I'm thinking, Bang Goes My Weekend.

The A&E staff put us all in a separate children's room with big plastic toys and shiny cube seating units that you sit on and slide straight off again, as if drunk. They take an X-ray of Lawrence's head and pronounce him fine.

'We're sorry to have wasted your time,' says Peter, making me feel somehow as though it was my idea.

'No, no: you did the right thing,' says the nurse.

They tell us to watch out for excessive drowsiness – in the baby – and we restart our journey to my mother's. I spend most of the journey worrying that she'll blame me.

8 Two's a Crowd

I get a reminder about my smear test. The Margaret Pyke Centre is near the shops: I think, I'll make a day of it!

I waltz in, pramless, slingless and as irritatingly care-free as a girl in a san-pro ad.

'Just before I do it,' says the nurse, 'we always have to check that you're not pregnant.'

'Well!' I say. 'That *would* be a turn up! We're planning to have another one quite soon, but . . .'

'Shall we just do a test, to make sure?'

This time when I get the news, I'm alone. At least the nurse thinks it's funny too, so that helps. I can't wait to see the look on Peter's face.

'You're *not*!'

'I bloody *am*. From 0 to 60 in five weeks, same as last time.'

'Cup of tea, or something stronger?'

'I'll tell you one thing, Mr Super Sperm. After this one, you're sleeping in the shed.'

'Hey, Lawrence, guess what?'

'You're going to have a little brother or sister!'

He doesn't say anything. He is, after all, six months old.

Outside I bump into my neighbour, Mira, who's just had her second.

'Hey! Guess what! I'm going to have another one too!' She turns sideways and edges through her gate.

'Well, I've got just one piece of advice,' she says. 'Enjoy life with just one while you can. Two is *not* one-plus-another-one: it's a *crowd*.' She makes this point a trifle over-emphatically, I think. Mind you, she only gave birth a few days ago. She's bound to be feeling a bit jaded.

'Two's a crowd, eh? Ha-ha! Well, OK!'

How right she is we can't even begin to appreciate.

We tell our friend Alison. The sibling rivalry, in her boys' case, is currently fuelled by pubescent surges of testosterone.

'The boys fight over *everything*. When I drove them to my parents' last week,' she says, 'they fought all the way. Connor said: *"Niall's looking out of my window!"'* She shakes her head.

Poor woman, I think, to have such petty, unreasonable kids. Then I remember what we were like.

My life was pretty wonderful for the first three years

until my sister ruined it, by being born. One moment the lovable toddler with dark curls and a nice line in chat, I was suddenly last year's model, in grey school pinafore and boyish, too-short fringe. My 'present from the baby', a hand-made bridal outfit, I ruined by refusing to pose for the camera without the little white bag I had chosen as an accessory: a loop-ended sanitary towel.

As everyone gathered to praise the blue-eyed wonder, cooing, *'Isn't your little sister beautiful?'* I felt utterly cheated. As soon as she could pinch finger and thumb together, I gave her a box of matches. Left alone with the scissors, I cut off her hair.

We fought over everything. Friends who came to play had to wait, baffled, while we held up their glasses of lemonade and scrutinized them for minuscule differences in the levels. Slices of cake were a forensic challenge, to be examined from every angle. Was that crumb sticking out a millimetre further than on the other piece? Space in the bath was measured using the tiles along the side: five tiles each, plus half the one in the middle. To avoid water fights – and potential drownings – the little chrome bridge that we kept the soap on was placed across as a divide. Mum would put it in position, then retreat, only to have to come back a minute later because one of us had nudged it, and the other was now shoving it back. The bedroom was like Belfast. Apple cores were lobbed over the bookcase that divided our territories. At night I flicked kirby grips over, then said in a scared voice: 'What was *that*?' Whereupon Claire, petrified, would whimper: 'I don't know!' If all went well, she would start crying.

By the time I had my first boyfriend, the bookcase barricade had been changed for a long, fitted desk unit we were supposed to *share*. As he and I looked longingly at each other, desperate to snog, Claire – now eleven – sat under the desk, reading a comic. Polite requests for her to piss off and die merely provoked the response of someone able to commit atrocities in full view of a UN Peacekeeping Force.

'It's my room too.'

'Well, it *is* her room too,' said Mum. We were always demanding she be fair, and now she was.

So as you can see, my life was utterly blighted. Feeble attempts to grab attention, such as publishing this book, are all part of my forty-year struggle to get back to that Eden when paradise was just me and two adults.

'Er, a bit late to go back now,' says Peter. 'I mean, unless you really don't want to have it.'

'No, I do. It's just that—'

'Hey, look on the bright side.'

'You always say that.'

'No, really. They'll be able to play together. They'll amuse each other and leave us in peace!'

'Maybe you're right.'

'Look at Sam and Joe (his nephews). They never argue.'

'They never *speak*.' (This is because they're naturally quiet, not because they hate each other.)

'Well, look at Jessica and me: we have a *great* relationship.'

'Yes, but when you were born, she was seven. She'd already had her life.'

'He won't remember a time without her; they'll be best friends.'

'They'll practically be twins.'

'We'll be able to re-use all this gear.'

'They'll be able to wear each other's clothes.'

'We'll be out of the tunnel sooner.'

'We'll *know* stuff.'

For every theory there's a counter-theory. Anyhow, whichever way we spin it, two facts remain: we wanted a second child, and we're having one. Bloody soon.

It's fun spreading the news. We love the way people gasp when we tell them. Like hovercrafts floating along on huge cushions of optimism, we're heady at the prospect of adventure.

Realizing I won't be able to carry the pair of them, I somehow believe I can *will* Lawrence to start walking before Number Two arrives. But thank God we are insanely optimistic, because without insane optimism you would never do anything at all. As Orson Welles said of making *Citizen Kane* at twenty-six: '*You succeed because you don't know all the things that can go wrong.*' And – when you're older, when you do know – he was asked, what do you do then? '*Continue in exactly the same way.*'

I book my Nuchal Fold scan and we get onto the really important thing: with our last few months of – relative – freedom, what should we do?

Looking ahead to a time when we might be a little less – flexible – than we are now, how should we make the most of this precious time? We've had our holiday of a lifetime already – to Tobago. But wait! In my anoraky capacity for hoarding things, I've never spent the Air Miles.

'What Air Miles?'

'That came with the video!'

'But that was ages ago.'

'I know! Let's see how far they stretch!'

We get out a map.

'Dublin.'

'Hmm. Bit cold.'

'Vienna.'

'Nah. Too – Austrian.'

'Italy. No, wait, just the north.'

'Milan? Can we get there?'

'Yep. But what's in Milan?'

'Giuseppe and Ortensia!'

'Right, that's it.'

They're old, dear friends of his. We ring them and tell them our two pieces of good luck: another baby, *and* Air Miles.

'With the baby?' says Giuseppe dryly.

'As good as.'

We pack our bags for a long weekend. They even have – despite not being parents yet themselves – a spare cot and pram. We put Lawrence in the sling, with our special back-up feeding kit of pre-measured formula that we mix into the bottle of water only when needed. If Lawrence sleeps for several hours, which he generally does in the sling, we won't have bottles of milk going off. This is brilliant! We're going abroad! With our baby! And not even that much luggage! We lock up and leave the spare keys with Dave, who is painting Lawrence's room. He's doing it in pink. I had a pink room as a child and Lawrence-plus-whoever will be bound to love it.

As we line up to go through to Departures, we can't help feeling a little smug.

'We're going to It-a-ly!'

'La, la-la, la, laa!'

At Passport Control we hold out our passports.

'Thank you, Sir, Madam. And where's the other one?'

'Other one?'

'For the baby.'

'Sorry?'

'Without a valid passport, the baby cannot travel.'

'What? But he's supposed to be on mine!'

'But he isn't, is he? We forgot.'

Our passports are whisked out of sight. Two men from Special Branch appear, and lead us away.

We are ushered into an office. Politely, but without undue friendliness, they ask us who the baby is.

'He's ours!' we say innocently. 'He's Lawrence Calman-Grimsdale.'

'Can you prove that?'

'Er . . .'

British Airways Flight 271 to Milan boards, and takes off. They show us several sheets of paper, stapled together.

'We've got the names of 3,000 babies here, who've been taken out of the country without permission.'

'It's usually one of the parents, isn't it?' I say knowledgeably.

'Yes, generally a foreign national.'

'I know, because my dad's girlfriend did a TV drama about it.'

I forget that we're in police custody, and think we're at a party.

'Did she, madam.'

'Look,' said Peter. 'We are really, really sorry about this. You clearly have more important things to do.'

'That's no problem, sir. We're not in any hurry.'

'We *are* really, really sorry, we truly are,' I add. I've been saving those Air Miles for six years.

'The thing is,' one of them said finally. 'If the airline carries a passenger illegally, they can be fined £10,000.'

'So, understandably,' adds the other, 'they like to be sure.'

We wait – for what, we don't know. Lawrence continues to sleep peacefully in the sling. We have two pre-measured pots of formula and two bottles of boiled water to mix them in. But it occurs to me that if he wakes up and can be breastfed, it might help our case. On the other hand, it seems mean to wake him up. And if I don't have enough milk yet, which is likely, they'll definitely think he isn't my child. I debate this with myself while we continue apologizing. Why don't they invite us to give up our plans for the weekend and piss off home? Maybe they're bored with terrorists and drug smugglers, and welcome the change of routine.

'Do you have the baby's birth certificate?' one of them asks casually.

'Not here, sadly. It's in the drawer at home. HANG ON!!' I leap up, nearly bashing Lawrence's head on the policeman's chin.

'Steady on, madam.'

'Dave the painter's there! Peter! He can fax it!! Would you accept a *fax*?!'

'Would you accept a fax?' repeats Peter, calmly.

'We will enquire as to whether that would be acceptable, yes.'

'I know where it is!'

'Calm down,' says Peter.

'You're always saying I don't know where things are. I do!'

The second detective returns – we hadn't noticed him slipping away – and says that if a fax were to be sent, it would be considered. It's up to British Airways, really: it's their £10,000. They point me towards a phone (we are pre-mobile) and I ring the house.

'Dave! How's it going?'

'Not bad. I've done all the walls and I'm just starting on the paintwork. It's quite a strong pink. It's for a girl, is it?'

'No. I don't know. Look, Dave? We're still at the airport.'

'You've not gone to Italy, then?'

'Not yet, no. Could you – Lawrence's birth certificate is in the dresser drawer, in the kitchen. Could you – possibly – get it, and fax it to the number I'm going to give you?'

'I don't think so.'

'Why?!'

'I've never used a fax.'

'It's terribly simple, honestly. Can you get the certificate, and I'll tell you what to do?'

'Er – OK.'

He finds it.

'You see?' I tell Peter. 'I do know where things are.'

We gather round the machine to watch the document emerge. Luckily, that patterned pink background they use hasn't turned it all grey; it is legible. And right at the bottom, after the Name, Place of Birth and so on, is a line in much smaller type I have never noticed before: 'WARNING: THIS CERTIFICATE IS NOT EVIDENCE OF THE IDENTITY OF THE PERSON PRESENTING IT.'

We look at each other and say nothing. Perhaps they won't read the small print.

They take the fax away, and after several agonizing minutes, return.

'You are free to travel,' says one.

'The fact that he has both your names has worked in your favour,' said the other.

'Great! Thank you! *Thank you!*'

'But our flight's gone.'

'That's no problem, sir. We can put you on another flight.'

'I'm afraid we're on Air Miles,' I blurt out guiltily.

'We're going to return you to the departure lounge. If you'd like to come to the British Airways desk, they'll give you an overnight pack.'

'Overnight pack?!'

'Yes. You may not be able to collect your luggage in Milan until tomorrow. It has been removed from the plane, but we're not absolutely sure when it will travel.'

'Oh. OK. Thanks!' We're only going for three days. Still, at least we are going. And I now have an excuse to buy some Italian clothes.

At the British Airways desk, we're given a plastic bag each, containing a toothbrush, paste, comb and plain white T-shirt.

'Hey! A free T-shirt!' I sit down to examine my gift.

'Would you like one with a razor?' asks the man. I feel my leg. 'You shouldn't be here *that* long.'

'Here are your boarding cards. You're on Flight 275,

which leaves at 15.10. You'll hear the announcement. We've rung Milan and told them to expect you.'

'Goodbye. And thank you!'

'That's quite all right, sir.'

'As for coming back, well . . .'

'You'll have to show the fax again and hope for the best.'

They melt away and, as if on cue, Lawrence stirs and wakes up.

'Actually,' I say, 'I think they realized we were incompetent, rather than criminal.'

'Yes, very.'

It is the week before half-term, and the plane is about a third full. We have two stewardesses each, and another offers to walk Lawrence up and down the aisle while we have our drinks.

But at Linate we find ourselves in a small, crowded office, facing an official behind a desk. We present our fax.

'In London—' we begin.

He slaps the fax with the back of his hand, as if trying to stun a fish.

'*London!*' He implies it's a preposterous place where people cross borders with flimsy sheets of paper: not a proper city like his. He's having none of it.

'Oh. Well, d'you think—'

'You sit. I phone *London*.'

We sit. The room is filled with officials, all smoking. I've forgotten how much smoke one cigarette can produce. Four or five going at once and the air is opaque. Lawrence stirs again in the sling. I've probably built up enough milk by now for a feed, and figure if I feed him myself, they'll surely see he's my child and let us go. On the other hand, we could all choke to death before I even get my tits out.

'I need to feed the baby,' I announce boldly.

'You go in there.'

I am ushered into a tiny side office, mercifully free of smoke. Peter remains, smiling un-nervously to show he isn't a child abductor.

After about an hour, the official finds the line to London engaged for the umpteenth time, and drops the phone back onto the desk.

'It's busy. You go.'

'What? We can leave?'

'Yes, yes. Go.'

We scuttle away before he changes his mind. I have no idea how, since we're about five hours late, but Giuseppe is there to meet us.

*

Lawrence enjoys his trip, particularly the Sunday afternoon which he spends screaming. And something wonderful happens.

'He's slept through the night!'

Travel seems to agree with him. We stand over the cot and gaze at him, as if he will look different.

We return from our adventure to find his room duly painted, even if it is a somewhat more *Barbie-ish* pink than we remember from the colour chart. We'll probably end up with another boy: fine. When they're old enough to have a say about the colour, they can repaint it themselves.

At about three months, just as last time, I start falling asleep twice a day, and feeling sick. But I discover a brilliant cure: food! You know that traditionally morning sickness puts you *off* eating. You also know that things with ginger in often make it slightly better. But – selflessly using myself as guinea pig – I have found that tiny morsels of *anything* alleviate it to the point where normal life can resume. The only problem is, the effect wears off rather soon. I have to eat my own weight in biscuits every day.

Lawrence babbles, '*Da-da-da-da*' so we ring my mother and hold out the phone, whereupon he stops. He can nearly sit up, but just when you think he's stable, does a terrifying whiplash movement with his upper torso which sends his head flailing forward. If we put him within two miles of the coffee table, he will knock himself out, and quite possibly lose an eye. We make one concession to safety, and stash the coffee table away. We briefly consider getting cupboard clips, but the people we know who have them can never get their cupboards open easily, and anyhow, even when he does become mobile, he doesn't pull all the plates onto the floor. Instead, he opens them and peers in rather politely, as if seeing round the house, then closes them again.

A friend with a daughter the same age invites us to one of those groups I hate, called *Tick-Tock* or *Humpty-Dumpty*. As I am still hoping to turn into the sort of person who likes – or can at least tolerate – sitting on a cold church-hall floor chanting, '*Hickory-dickory-dock*,' we go along. Lawrence isn't interested. He only wants to crawl across the middle of the neat baby circle and snatch the others' maracas.

I always believed that women couldn't be creepy, but that was before encountering people who perform for the under-fives. This one clearly has favourites, who get to be the mice while she chases them with a cardboard cleaver. The effect is clearly meant to be jolly, but she comes over to me like Jack Nicholson in *The Shining*. Then she goes round handing out shakers and bells and so on to each child. But she misses out Lawrence. And although he's oblivious, I gasp as though I've been winded. She has passed over *My Child*! Right, that's it! You people who dress up as mice and pretend to run up clocks have had your chance.

Number Two swims through its Nuchal Fold scan and blood test, and somersaults through the twenty-week scan. As before, we've decided not to know the gender, but go for the Mystery Parcel option.

'Actually it's our policy not to reveal the sex,' explains the radiographer. 'For one thing, even at twenty weeks you can get it wrong.'

'And some people . . . certain – cultures – don't want certain sexes. For example, girls.'

'Er, well, yes.'

As spring turns to summer, I put on the same two bits of maternity wear as the year before, a black top and bright orange skirt, so if I go into labour while I'm out, I'll be easy to find in a crowd. At the cinema one evening, we're greeted by friends we haven't seen for a year.

'Haven't you had that baby yet? Surely it must be ready by *now*!'

But as Peter's father used to say, Laughing leads to Crying.

My mother says solemnly one evening: 'I've been observing Lawrence, and he doesn't respond to music.'

'What kind of music? Jazz? Classical? Deep House?'

'I sang to him, and he didn't respond. I think you should get his hearing tested. Properly.'

'He's fine,' I say. 'He's *fine*.'

She goes back home, and I dissolve into a puddle of worry.

'She thinks he's deaf! What are we going to do?!'

'I'm sure he isn't.'

'He just doesn't respond to *her*.'

'Well nor do you,' says Peter. 'Maybe it runs in the family. Still, isn't he supposed to have his ears tested about now anyway?'

Lawrence is the right age, eight months, yet the invitation from the health visitor hasn't come. To appease my mother, and because I secretly fear she might be right – a *truly* horrendous possibility – I ring the Audiology Department of the local NHS Trust.

A week later we are seen. After a two-hour wait, during which Lawrence gets more and more bored and restless, and I get more and more tense and anxious, we go in. The doctor is some kind of senior paediatrician, with a nurse. She tells me to sit Lawrence on my lap, and says: 'He's not sitting up very well, is he?'

'He's – well, he's – I don't know,' I say weakly. I have a feeling this is not going to go well.

I am right. The nurse waves a couple of building blocks at him, while the doctor goes behind us and claps her hands. Lawrence decides he's more interested in the blocks. Even after several goes, he shows no inclination to turn round.

'You do realize,' says the doctor, 'that this child is *Developmentally Delayed*.' And she writes it down. So *that's* why he didn't turn round, I realize now; he knew she was a Horrid Lady.

At that moment, however, I can't tell you what happens because the blood drains out of my head and I start to cry. Even as I carry him to the car – my bright, bouncing, alert little boy – I know she is wrong. I'm almost more angry with myself than with her, for not telling her where to shove her pencil. And her fucking building blocks. From the moment we arrived she had a bitter, resentful look on her face. Did I resemble the woman who'd stolen her husband? The mother who'd never cuddled her? Did she just not like my face? I don't like it myself that much, but still: a person has rights. Last week, a bit of work came in, and I rang up to try and get an alternative time. That's it! I'm being punished for Putting My Career First. I've been *branded*. As far as she's concerned, Lawrence is Deaf and Stupid, and I am Evil.

As soon as I get back I ring Peter, who struggles to follow my account.

'Sh-sh-she s-s-s-said h-h-he (sob, splutter, sob).'

'I can't – what? You poor thing! Calm down. Of course he's not deaf. Of course he's not. I'll see you tonight. Everything'll be fine, I promise.'

How? Our child has been tested and *failed*. It's on his *record*. So what if this woman would have sacked the staff of Colditz for being too soft. She has the final say. And worst of all, I initiated it! If I hadn't listened to *my mother*, if I'd just gone to Carol the Health Visitor, who is *nice*, it wouldn't have happened. I pour my heart out to Maureen, the neighbours, the plumber, the man in the Turkish supermarket and every other person I meet.

Maureen dismisses the whole thing with a gentle shake of her head. Not prone to displays of outrage, she gives me to understand that such notes are not worth the official paper they're stamped upon. Nonetheless I spend the next week in a state of volatile gloom. How can I have another baby when things are going as badly as this?

I tell my neighbour, Mira, who's as far away from anyone's idea of a Bad Mother as it is possible to get. Well, I never hear her shouting.

'Oh, mine failed that thing too,' she says airily. 'Lots of them do.'

'*Really?!*' I have to stop myself from crumpling at the knees and wiping my eyes on her skirt.

'Of course! It's totally unscientific.'

I start to feel better. Then I bump into Kath, whose son Roman is exactly Lawrence's age.

'It's total bollocks,' she says firmly.

'Why do they do it then?'

'Oh, it's something to tick off in that stupid red book. Sweep it from your mind. Oh, and while you're at it, throw out all your books.'

'My *books*???!'

'Your *baby* books. They're just full of things to make you worry. A friend told me to get rid of mine, and I've never looked back.'

I return home with renewed purpose. Lawrence isn't alone! Others 'fail' too! Intelligent ones! Ones with Better Parents than us. Ones who get into Good Schools. Ones who – hang on: if The System is relying on something so patently unscientific, as Mira puts it, how can its credibility remain unchallenged? How can we believe in It? Is it possible that we could – should – put more faith in ourselves? The thrilling – and terrifying – prospect presents itself: *we might know something*. We might even, at times, *know more than It*.

I call Suzy, the one who was able to go to the loo because we gave her a mobile to hang from her baby's cot. He's seven now.

'How're you going, Suze?'

'Fine. I'm pregnant.'

'Wow! So that's – three!'

'Four.'

'By the way . . . Did yours pass their Distraction Test?'

'Their what? I dunno. I can't remember.'

'What?! *Really*?' God, she's cool.

'Oh, I'm terrible. I *never* fill out that stupid red book. And you know what? When the health visitor comes—'

'What?'

'I hide.'

'You what?'

'Sure! I hide behind the curtains, and the kids tell me when she's gone.'

I put Lawrence in the playpen with his Aston Martin and get down the baby books. Into a box I put *What to Expect When You're Expecting*, with its bumper load of things to worry about in each trimester, *What to Expect The First Year*, with its generous helping of things to fail at in each month of development, the two big, floppy breastfeeding books by Sheila Kitzinger, and the pristine *Baby and Toddler Meal Planner* by Annabel Karmel, a present from my mother, who fed us out of jars.

I keep only one, the *Book of Child Care* by Dr Hugh Jolly, as it says: *'The "experts" should not be regarded as infallible; It is up to you to be selective about other people's advice ... Make decisions based on your own instincts.'* Keep it? I'll bloody frame it.

9 Unfaithful to Lawrence

As I get bigger, it's becoming much harder to pick Lawrence up, and of course there is the decision we made to live in a house composed almost entirely of stairs.

'I'm sure by the time the second one's born, he'll be able to walk,' I say to anyone who visits. Strangely, they all look sceptical. In fact, he does start – but recreationally, like people who take their car out on Sundays for a spin. He hasn't actually got it in mind to go anywhere. And somehow I have got being *able* to walk confused with *wanting* to. I try to get him to increase his distances, to practise as much as possible before the big day, but time is not on our side. He still likes to be picked up as much as usual, and of course, to be carried up to bed. At least being eight months gone gets me out of this. Peter agrees to help me even further by not going away for work – or out at all – for the next five years.

Peter and I decide to start Lawrence on full days at

Maureen's a bit before that, so he doesn't feel displaced by the new one. Again, I go on to Peter about how guilty I feel. And again, I am incredibly grateful for the help. In fact, without Maureen in the frame we wouldn't have considered having the other one so soon.

On 4 November, our agreed date – to avoid Bonfire Night – Peter and I arrive at the hospital.

'We're really sorry,' says a nurse. 'Only there's a woman in theatre, and she's haemorrhaging, so . . . could you come back tomorrow? We're awfully sorry.'

'You mean someone's bleeding to death in my slot? Cheek!' We reassure her that we do *not* mind, and go for coffee.

'What shall we do?'

'We've got an extra day!'

'Ooh, like free time on the meter.'

We go and see *The Truman Show*, which seems appropriate, as Truman is a kind of permanent baby who has never left the womb. When he does try to escape, he finds his whole world is a set.

'It's a great idea,' I say. 'If the children show signs of trying to be independent too early, we could—'

'What, paint a sign saying "Squat" on the garden shed?'

'I'm just saying.'

'Look, let's just get this one born, shall we?'

We return the next day, 5 November. Baby 2 is born to the same opera duet, in the same sociable atmosphere. In an exact replay, Peter moves down to where the action is and gasps, 'It's a girl!'

She is called Lydia. There are no breathing problems, and she comes upstairs with me, where a friendly midwife offers me my own room.

'You back again already?'

'I like the view.'

'Put your stuff in there. You get your own loo.'

'Great! Aren't you supposed to pay or something?'

'They're for twins and multiples, but we haven't got any. You get a spare bed as well.'

'Can I have friends to stay?'

'Yeah, if you keep fairly quiet.'

I've got my own sink, as well as the loo, and a spare bed for the beer and takeaways which Peter will bring later. I unload my nappies, chocolate and magazines. From the window, I can see some of the lives I didn't lead. Across the road is RADA, where my best friend Tilly and I went to giggle at Anton Lesser when he was a student and we were silly fourteen-year-olds. She became an actor, I didn't. Just behind us is UCL, where my sister went to university; I didn't. Right at the end is the building where my father lived; on his sixtieth birthday he urged us to have children. But he died two years later, and never knew that we'd listened. Now here I am: a mother of two, with a life that wasn't on the list.

Lydia is asleep in the plastic wheely cot beside me. I listen to the distant fireworks for a while, then fall asleep. Tomorrow, Peter is bringing Lawrence.

But I'm dreading seeing him. I feel as though by having another baby, I've been unfaithful. I'm convinced I've betrayed him. Why did no one warn me about this? I lie in my nicely appointed room, gazing over the rooftops, feeling a total shit.

The next day, Peter brings him. I'm expecting a huge bollocking: *'How could you?!'* Then I remember he can't speak.

'Here's your new baby sister,' says Peter.

He does his fourteen-month-old drunk-style toddle, holding onto the seats of chairs, over to the bed, and peers at her, an unfamiliar expression on his face. Then he puts his head very gently on her tummy.

That's the sibling rivalry issue solved, then.

Peter would make a good mule. His look of clean-cut, unimpeachable integrity belies the fact that his Boots carrier contains two chicken jalfrezis and a large Budvar. We sit on the beds, have supper and talk. Back home, his sister is looking after Lawrence.

*

The day we bring Lydia home, Karen the midwife comes with us to 'help her settle in', i.e. mitigate the shock of being a Family of Four.

'Whatever happens,' I say to Peter, 'we are not getting a people mover.' He agrees, but transport is an Issue.

At first, I wheel Lawrence in the buggy, to Maureen's, the shops and so on, with Lydia in the sling. We have a new buggy to replace the pram – well not exactly new; Peter found it in the street. But it's a Chicco, a good brand, and with the mould scrubbed off, looks fine. But Lydia, who's having no trouble feeding, gets bigger. And heavier.

'I should be pleased, I know, because the feeding's so much easier than last time. But . . .' I unwrap her and flop into a chair.

'There's nothing for it,' says Peter. 'We have to—'

'Don't say it!'

'Yes! We have to get a Double Buggy.'

The double buggy, as I know from my prenatal on-street observation, is the foot-powered equivalent of the Humvee. It takes up whole pavements, forcing pedestrians to leap into the traffic. It brings out the belligerence in people. It should have its own licence.

I go round to Mira's for a test drive. She has the forward-and-back model, designed for combined upright-toddler-and-baby-sleepage. It's much narrower, but the baby goes behind, putting the much bigger weight at the front. Trying to get it up a kerb is like pushing a small van.

'Awful, isn't it?' She's right. You need the upper-arm strength of a docker. And even then you're still in the road, struggling, while lorries skid round you.

'I'll think about it.'

'Well, let me know if you solve it.'

'I probably will – by the time they're old enough to drive.'

We revert to our habitual mode when facing a dilemma: inertia. A couple of weeks later, another neighbour appears at the door.

'Would you like this? Only Mira said you might want one.'

'A double McLaren! How incredibly generous! Are you sure?'

'Oh, yes.' She rolls her eyes. 'I've gone on for as long as I can stand it.'

'I know what you mean.'

'There is one advantage to this particular model, though.'

'Cruise control?'

'It's actually slightly narrower than standard. So you can get into more places.'

'Like to buy food?'

'Providing your children aren't too—'

'Chubby.'

'Well, yes. Or you have to jam them in and it's hard to get them out. And each side does lie right back. So you can use it before six months, and one of them—'

'Or both . . .'

'Or both – can go to sleep.'

I ring Peter to share the exciting news. Luckily, I have no idea how heavy two children can be, even on wheels. Sleeping, their weight seems to double. Maybe that's why they call it a Double Buggy.

Now my life revolves entirely around which places I can get the DB into. I can no longer go into the community garden and watch people planting their mini allotments. The only stall at the market I can reach is the one at the end, which sells batteries. The bank is up a flight of steps and has *no cash machine*. Helen, my friend with three, has actually had to leave her bank and join a flatter one. Months of turning up with passports and moving sixteen direct debits, all because she didn't leave a proper gap between kids. I stand on the pavement and gaze resentfully into the Turkish supermarket which has hitherto catered to all my needs. As they only ever open one of their double doors, I am now banned. I can, however, still get into the homosexual shop that sells candlesticks, vases and throws.

'Hi,' says Peter. 'What's for supper?'

'A set of espresso cups.'

'. . .'

'They're really nice, though. Look at the shape.'

The next morning he gets up at seven and goes to Sainsbury's, which is why I married him.

10 The Swingometer

Lawrence has got a word: *badu*. He uses it for a variety of occasions, a bit like the French use *alors*. We take him to Hampstead Heath to practise his walking, in a purple padded suit. From a distance he looks like an animated bilberry.

'God, you can tell he's a bloke.'

'Why?'

'When we got in just now, I said: "Would you like your bottle?" and he went over to his usual spot on the sofa. Like his seat in the pub.'

'Aah. And Lydia's such a girl.'

'Why do you say that?'

'She does incredibly smelly farts, just like you.'

In the weeks coming up to Christmas, Lawrence is sick quite a bit, screams the place down when Peter takes him to the doctor's for amoxycillin, and then is suddenly better. His new achievement, going up and down stairs, is augmented by his abnormally high intelligence:

'Lawrence – can you turn round and come back?'

'He did! Look!'

'Amazing!'

Peter's sister Jessica, mother of two grown-up boys, comes round with some of their old toys.

'Lawrence, where's the car?' (There it is!)

'Where's your *blue* car?' (There it is!)

'Put the phone in your other hand.'

'He did it! He did it!'

Our son is clearly incredibly gifted. We can only hope that, when the time comes, there is a school extraordinary enough to accommodate him. Of course, *we're* not competitive. But some people . . .

My old friend Mandy invites us round for coffee. Lawrence and her son were born in the same week. The idea is that she and I will enjoy some adult company with each other while the children play. But the children are nearly two, which is the age of highest maintenance, and so after an hour we are still trying to finish the one sentence. Also, I have Lydia with me, so the scene is Joyce Grenfell meets Mike Leigh.

'Well, don't hit her and she won't hit you! Anyway, I had this idea for a – can you give it back, please? Give it *back*! Lawrence, give me back my pen. No. Don't *do* that!

'Now, what toys have you got? Well . . . why don't we read Lydia's first, then – what have I told you about throwing books? Is it too early for a drink? Just sit down there. Not on *top* of her. (Sigh.) No, *there*! So are you thinking of going back to BBC Scot—? Right, leave her *alone*! I'm *coming*! Well, if you do that, of course it'll spill. Don't cry. I'm not shouting. I'M NOT SHOUTING!'

Mandy has invited another woman, Elisabeth, a Swiss – sort of Amazon, tall and blonde – who is clearly very intelligent. In fact, I wonder, after being in her orbit for an hour, whether she might be *too* intelligent. After all, with toddlers, you do have to reset your coordinates a bit.

She wants her daughter Lena to be bilingual, but poor old Lena's never fast enough. Her mother barks: '*Ein, zwei, drei!*' – over and over again.

'Ein, zwei, drei,' mumbles Lena, or something like it. (It could be: 'I'm not dry.') Elisabeth looks at us. Are we supposed to repeat it too? She's so scary I almost do. Then she starts on about Lena's inadequate Gross Motor Skills. Gross Motor Skills, as every mother knows, means stuff like walking, while Fine Motor Skills is picking your nose. And Lena has just turned one. Can you remember when you learned to walk? Did it ever come up at a job interview? Can you actually walk *better* than someone who learned six months later than you? I stumble home, flattened.

'*Why?*' I ask Peter that night.

'Not enough to do.'

'What do you mean?! Looking after a child – or in my case *two* (I give him a pointed look) – is exhausting! How can you—'

'Nah, nah. I mean she's bored, needs stimulation, needs—'

'To go back to work?'

Maybe he has a point. After many years in the pressured but highly stimulating world of international whatever, poor old Elisabeth is suddenly at home all day with someone whose intellectual capacity is measured by the ability to shout 'Doggie!' when catching sight of any animal smaller than a whale. It takes some adjusting to. And then there's the fact that motherhood is impossible to evaluate. You've got no way to measure your progress and therefore no sense of achievement. No sooner have you fed them, changed their nappies or picked all the squashed petits pois out of the carpet, than it's time to do it again. No one comes in and says: '*Right, so you've done tidying, rocking them to sleep, persuading them to eat a fish finger – you can now do something else.*' You do not *move on*. The only thing that can be said for the physical drudgery is that it at least makes you too knackered to care whether your child is 'ahead'.

I escape for a drink with my friend Mark, one of the links with my Former Life. He has no children – yet.

'That's nothing,' he says. 'My brother-in-law talks to all his children as if they're the Nobel Prize Committee.'

'How old are they?' I ask.

'Jack's only five. He can't even swallow a simple morsel of sea bass in fennel without his father demanding to know its progress. ' *"And where's it going now, Jack? That's right! The – oesophagus."* '

'Ah, poor little thing!'

'Nah. He's just as bad. If you ask him a question, he answers, ' *"I think you'll find . . ."* '

I am reminded of this on a visit to my mother's, when Lawrence helps me get money out of the cash machine. I hold him up and start reciting the buttons he needs to press: 'Sev-en . . . two-o . . . six . . .' I am about to shout 'eight!' when Peter points out that the whole of Folkestone can hear. By the way, for thieves reading at home, this is not my actual PIN.

Lydia is five months old, and Lawrence has taught himself to put in her dummy. He has expanded his vocabulary beyond *'badu'*. The most useful word is *Mummy*, because it means *'Want it NOW'*.

Lydia goes to Maureen's for a trial day, and Lawrence is furious when she picks her up and he is relegated to second cuddle.

'So the sibling rivalry problem that we avoided by having them so close together . . .'

'Is now her problem?'

'That's OK then.'

I've started crying after leaving Lawrence at Maureen's: I don't know why. *Then*, the next time I leave Lydia I discover that the older sister of one of the other boys is suddenly being left there as well, on days when she doesn't feel like going to school. And her mother's a teacher! This puts Maureen 'over the limit'. I know she can cope, but I'm angry with her for not telling us, and angry with the other family for taking advantage.

Peter says: 'It'll be fine.'

'Well, I'm not leaving Lydia then. I can't.'

'It'll be fine.'

'Will you stop saying that? Just say something helpful or fuck off.'

While I'm worrying myself into a frazzle about how to handle it, Kath — my favourite mother there — talks to Maureen on behalf of us both. This is a relief, because I have discovered I am hopeless at this sort of thing. God only knows what I'm going to do when they start school. I express this concern to Peter, who says: 'It'll be fine.'

A week before Christmas, Lawrence wobbles off the landing and falls down the stairs. The sound — like someone emptying a sack of potatoes — is terrible. But his head doesn't hit the tiles at the bottom. I'm too scared to look, but there is only a little red mark. I tell my sister, who berates me for not getting a stairgate.

'*We* never had a stairgate.'

'We lived in a flat.'

My emotions are in tatters. One moment Lawrence is charmingly pushing his trolley round the kitchen, and reversing skilfully. The next thing we know, he is screaming his head off, clinging piteously to Peter when being put in his cot, and hurling his toys out with great force. While being dressed, he head-butts me from behind, so hard that I shout, 'How *dare* you?!'

He's advanced all right: at sixteen months he's starting on the Terrible Twos. I write in my notebook: *Is this the end of the World's Most Charming Child?*

I've always been volatile, subject to dreadful swings in the space of moments. But this is crazy. To a cinema fan like me it's a bit like watching a scene from *A Night at the Opera* followed by one from *Schindler's List*. Then it's *Mad Max*, then *A Night at the Opera*, then *Schindler's List* again, over and over again. I feel as though I'm being pumped full of uppers and downers.

Lawrence has started throwing his head back while being given his dinner. Peter – almost arbitrarily – gives him some baked beans on a spoon, and Lawrence puts them straight into his mouth. He *is* a genius!

'D'you think we should have given him the spoon before?'

'I'm sure we should, but it's so bloody messy.'

Having put away three spoonfuls, Lawrence is eating the remaining beans individually from the table.

'Look at those Fine Motor Skills.'

The next time we do it, he throws the beans straight onto the table.

'So development's not, like, a linear thing.'

'It's more of a spread out, all over the table and floor thing.'

Peter has a brainwave. He takes one spoon and Lawrence the other. That way, for every load that goes onto the table, we get one into his mouth.

'Darling, you are clever!'

The *next* time we feed him, he dips the spoon into the rice and chicken, then scrunches the food with his hand as if washing it.

On New Year's Eve he has a sip of champagne. In January he takes his first proper walk – of three steps – with a very light tread, a bit like a Thunderbirds puppet. We go to Dorset, and we walk hand in hand on the deserted beach, while Peter drags Lydia in the pushchair through the sand. Lawrence is quite a chunk, with golden curls; imagine a piano mover in a Shirley Temple wig. But when we take him out of the bath, hair all wet, he looks like Michael Caine as the sleazy agent in *Little Voice*.

Now he is displaying a worrying tendency towards some kind of gender confusion. In the bath he tells me:

'My baby's asleep.' But there's no doll around.

'Where is it?' I ask him.

'In my tummy.'

One morning he gets conjunctivitis and wakes up with his eyes stuck shut. As he was busy wiping snot into them all night, we are not surprised.

Lydia's gaze follows me round the room. She has movie-star lips and my mother's slightly flat-ended nose. She's so beautiful I wonder why the other mothers don't just spit in my face. Maybe I can cope with ageing, deterioration and death after all. Then she throws her tummy in the air and screams at me, and I think: No, I can't.

Feeding her is going far better than it even did with Lawrence – her not being in an incubator and my eating properly does help – and I am delighted by the convenience of it. Invited to a wedding by one of Peter's ex-colleagues, we set off with that ominous spring in the step that almost always precedes a major embarrassment of some sort. The reception is at the Orangery in Holland Park, a narrow conservatory jammed with standing people. I have to find a waiter to find me a chair so I can feed Lydia, while Peter dashes outside every three minutes to retrieve Lawrence, who has gone rather suddenly from being unsteady on his feet to being *fast*. Outside the reception is an entire park with a hundred directions to run in, and he is evidently planning to try them all. I finally get the chair and sit down with Lydia, bodies pressed around us as on a crowded tube, only to remember that my lovely flowery dress undoes at the back. So to achieve full breast access, I have to unzip the whole thing pretty much to the waist. This is the sight that confronts Peter's former boss, a tall, boffiny type who I remember from a previous meeting is (a) extremely shy, and (b) somewhat uncomfortable in the presence of women.

Having pushed his way through the crowd, he says: 'Hello,' after which there is a dramatic pause before he takes in the fact that I am topless. Unable to retreat easily due to the density of the crowd, and evidently not wanting to seem rude, he hovers on tiptoe, eyes averted, muttering: 'And are you – er, ah – writing much?'

After Peter has fetched Lawrence for the twenty-fifth time we repair to the sandpit, where, with carefully concealed flutes of champagne, we discover you can take two children under two to a posh, stand-up party – if you're prepared to compromise. It's just a matter of choosing which things to compromise on, and it needn't be the champagne. We go home feeling we've coped quite well, even if our clothes are full of sand.

One Sunday we have lunch in Oxford with Antonia, an old swimming friend of mine. I say 'swimming friend'; I first met her lighting up a cigarette in the changing-rooms, explaining that she'd been dragged there by Iris, a friend who had to exercise in the water because she had only one leg.

'I hate fucking swimming,' she muttered between drags. She and Iris were both pushing seventy. They invited me for coffee, and gave me their views on child-rearing. I had none at this point – children, not views. Antonia and her daughter Eleanor, Eleanor's boyfriend and their daughter Araminta all shared a house, along with a gay, black film-maker, a freelance illustrator and a changing assortment of others.

'You know why Araminta's so well behaved?' said Antonia, puffing away. 'Because half the time, her parents can't be bothered with her.'

'Well, surely . . . I mean—'

'The other day, I came in and what d'you think I

found? Araminta bawling in her pushchair, on the landing. And where was Eleanor? Upstairs, at her desk!'

'Oh yes,' added Iris, though with approval or disapproval I couldn't tell.

'I said, "Eleanor, *what are you doing?*" And she said, "Mother, if you must know, I couldn't get the buckle undone on the bloody thing, and I had a deadline, so I left her there." Really!'

'Oh yes,' repeated Iris.

'But you see, this is why Minty's so well behaved.'

And sure enough, when we arrive at the house, Minty greets us charmingly, and offers to show Lawrence and Lydia her toys. Lydia survives the outing unscathed, but Lawrence trips and snaps part of his front tooth off on the step. He recovers from this far sooner than I do. How did I manage to let *that* happen? I decide it's Peter's fault, for taking half a Sunday off – which he never does – to meet someone from work. When we get home, I help take our minds off it by teaching Lawrence to help me load the dishwasher. Lydia can now put her own dummy back in, so she's well on her way to independence.

Just before his second birthday Lawrence learns to say: 'No wannoo . . .' – the key phrase of this year, and henceforth our whole relationship.

11 I Do Something Right

With Lawrence at Maureen's I can concentrate for most of the day on one child. This even leads to brief spells of peace, during which I feel I am *'getting it right'*. One morning I allow myself a little shopping. In the cafe at John Lewis I put my coffee down, and park Lydia's buggy some distance from the table – *so I think* – while I get a glass of water. At last, I feel I've reached some sort of plateau. Things are going quite well, and—

Suddenly she rises up in her pushchair – like Glenn Close at the end of *Fatal Attraction* – grabs my coffee and throws it all over herself. As I take it black, it is very hot. I chuck my water over her, then take the water from someone else's table, marvelling at how quickly, in a crisis, a middle-class person can say, *'Excuse me, could I possibly take this? Thank you.'*

I tear her suit off. The John Lewis first-aid rep – *'I'm Sue, the First-Aid Rep'* – calls an ambulance and throws more cold water and ice all over her, so that she goes from screaming because she's covered in boiling hot stuff, to screaming because she's freezing cold. A towel appears from somewhere. The paramedics rush in with aloe vera gel which they smooth on, then wrap her in a kind of cling-film like 1980s disco wear. They put an oxygen mask on her and wheel her through huge corridors behind the sales floor, with me and the pushchair running behind. The siren wails all the way to UCH. As we jump the lights, I think: *Lawrence would have loved this.* At the vehicle entrance to A&E, three plastic surgeons are waiting. Maybe business is slow. I have given Lydia her dummy, which is pretty effective; she has stopped screaming and fallen asleep.

'I'm awfully sorry about this,' I say. 'She *was* screaming.'

'When did you throw the cold water on?' they ask.

'Er . . .'

'How soon after she spilled the coffee?'

'Twenty seconds? I'm really sorry, I'm not sure.'

They examine her whole front, paying particular attention to her pubic area.

'Did the coffee get down this far, can you remember?'

'No. It stopped about there.'

'Well, she's lucky. That area scars very badly, but you've saved her from being scarred anyway.'

'Really?'

'Yes. Every second before you put water on a burn like this makes a big difference.'

I've actually done something right! There should be a kind of tick, the opposite of points, that you can put on your Mothering Licence. Gold stars, maybe. I sit in a cubicle while they put on more aloe vera, fresh cling-film, and a wide bandage in which they cut arm holes to make a kind of vest. They also give me a mini bottle of formula with a disposable teat, as I have run out.

Back home, I tell Peter and Lawrence of our adventure.

'Well done you!' says Peter. The sense of having made a difference, a tangibly positive difference, is fantastic. Three days later we go back to have the dressing off. The skin is broken on one part of her tummy, but she is otherwise perfect. Five years on, she still loves to hear the story of Lydia and the Coffee.

The excitement never ends. Mira gives us a potty.

'It looks brand new,' I say. 'Don't you want it?'

'My children won't pee into anything red.'

Lawrence loves it, though more as a toy than an aid to actual toilet training. He associates it with weeing inasmuch as the two occasionally coincide, but as he is always sitting down at the time, the wee does not generally go in, or even near, the target. Mainly he likes to get my old doll, Champagne – a sixties chav in yellow miniskirt – and put her on it. Then he sits on top of her in a disconcerting suggestion of some kind of 18–30 Holiday party game, shouting: 'Wee wee!'

Afterwards he says, *'Aw-right?'* sounding exactly like Maureen's scaffolder husband, Ron. He also likes to take the pilot out of his Playmobil helicopter, and wipe his nether regions. I am getting nowhere with this 'training'. The only training going on is his training me to realize my own limitations.

'He'll do it when he's ready,' says Maureen.

'Children in Africa don't need toilet training,' says my mother in *Horizon* mode. 'They learn to do it all naturally.'

'Yes, but then they don't need to be toilet trained because they all die of Aids.'

'I'm just trying to be helpful.' Grandparents should have a phrase emblazoned on them like a council motto: *Working to undermine you.*

There's one thing I have trained Lawrence to do. When he hears a car hooting in the traffic, he says, 'Shit.'

Suddenly he starts speaking in sentences, like the Starship Enterprise going into warp drive.

'Do that again and you're in trouble,' he tells his teddy.

Lydia, ten months, is crawling, but of course we don't make a big deal of it because we've seen it all before. We make up for this by stopping dead in our tracks when she smiles her dazzling smile. Caught in the headlights Peter becomes completely useless.

'You'll forget to go to work if you're not careful.'

'Shut up: I love her now, not you.'

The Calman pedantry is showing up already. When Lawrence tells me: 'I saw a mixer lorry,' I say: 'Was it up the road?' He says: 'No: *down* the road.'

He does a pooh in the bath which is a talking point for days. It's not one of the Development Milestones as laid out in the little red book, but he feels a sense of achievement which we feel it would be churlish to undermine.

To train them to have the same taste as us – or at least not primary-coloured, *kiddie* taste – we take them to the Ken Adam exhibition at the Serpentine Gallery. There are video clips, drawings and stills from his best-known film sets, including *You Only Live Twice* and *Dr Strangelove*.

'Look, Lawrence: a spaceship!'

'A space chip: I eat it.'

'How long before we can show them a James Bond?' says Peter.

'How long before we can all go to the cinema together?'

There's another pressing issue. I'm scared that if I leave it too long, I'll forget how to work. Or how to be Out There. I want to be Out. I want to *go* somewhere, *be* someone again, a Person. I want to go on the tube and have coffee in a paper cup. I ring up a nice script-editor at the BBC, where they are interested in an idea of mine. He invites me to come and see him and the producer. Peter now has our friend Alison working for him, and they offer to mind Lydia while I have my meeting. I wheel Lydia in, to admiring glances, but also realize I am quite nervous. I get back on the tube.

In BBC reception a rather attractive man gives me a big, '*Are you free tonight?*' sort of smile. He looks a bit familiar, but I can't place him. I get to my meeting, but it starts late. Then, when the producer *does* appear, there are building works and we can't hear what we're saying. He makes a few calls to find another office, then we set off. When we get there, he gossips and chats with the nice script-editor, but no one mentions my actual script.

Eventually they get round to it. It is 4.30 and Maureen shuts down at 5.30. She *never* works late. I've got twenty-five minutes to get all the way back down the Westway and through King's Cross in the rush hour. If I grab Lydia and drive like a maniac I might, just might, not be late.

'So how's the pilot coming along, then?'

Mustn't be late for Maureen, mustn't be late for Maureen.

'Hm? Oh, fine. Fine.'

He tells me to do another draft. Sick with anxiety, I get to Peter and run along the corridors pushing Lydia like a rickshaw driver in the war escaping the Japanese. I reach Maureen with two minutes to spare, and resolve not to have another meeting for a long time, possibly never. It wasn't just the rushing; I realize I hated the feeling of being so far away. Still, I've remembered the name of the attractive man in reception.

'How was the meeting?' says Peter.

'Hopeless. But Gary Lineker smiled at me.'

'So the day wasn't entirely wasted.'

I decide to forget about having a career. On Sunday we go for a walk with Julia and her four children on Hampstead Heath, and Lawrence falls face-first into a huge clump of nettles. He is screaming, and in shock. We calm him, and hold him, and all the children gather dock leaves. But what really seems to help is shouting at the Sharp Plants.

'You're very naughty!' I tell them. 'Now just – *Go Away!*'

We have been looking for a babysitter, and think we have found one.

Sharon is a cheerful teenager who lives nearby and is instinctively good with kids, possibly because she's so much nearer their age. Also, being seventeen she doesn't collapse with exhaustion halfway through the day. Even better than that, she knows Maureen and is therefore part of the network of those women who allow the likes of me to swan about going on the radio and writing books. There are a few exceptions: those literary females who manage to create great works while being full-time mothers. Possibly they type with their nipples. But if it weren't for the Maureens and Sharons of the Western world, far fewer books, magazines, radio and TV shows would be produced. Which may indeed be no loss. But more women like me would also end up on street corners waving empty vodka bottles at strangers.

Maureen takes her summer holiday in June, throwing into disarray the working mothers of the two older boys who are now at school. It doesn't affect us – yet. In fact, it's to our advantage.

'Hey, let's go on holiday at the same time!'

'While it's cheaper, and there aren't millions of other families taking up all the—'

'Food.'

'Whatever.'

We book ten days in Menorca, in a resort that looks like a newly built suburb, surrounded by nothing. Sharon's uncomplicated approach is ideal for a baby and newly qualified toddler and a nearly two year old. We have a wild and crazy idea.

'Would you like to come on holiday with us?'

And thank God she says yes, as Lawrence – a keen walker – spends pretty much the whole ten days escaping across the hotel grounds and having to be brought back before he reaches the lifts. That leaves Peter and me to take turns swimming and minding Lydia, who sits in the shade in her pushchair sporting a 1920s-looking hat that covers everything except her enormous cheeks. The pool is nice, but the alienating ambience of the complex and the sudden dashes across the lawn to grab Lawrence put me in mind of *The Prisoner*. This feeling is compounded when we leave Sharon to babysit and find there is nowhere to go.

'Next time,' I say, 'I'll find a place with a town.'

'Or indeed anything.'

But this suits Sharon, who – even though she babysits

happily for us at home – gets sulky when we try to leave her alone with the kids. The nearest we get to a romantic night out is to leave them in their room with a pizza one evening while we enjoy the fried buffet alone. But even then our spirits are dampened somewhat by her asking what time we'll be back.

'I think what we've learned here,' says Peter, 'is to possibly leave the foreign travel alone for a few years.'

'Say, till they're at college.'

'By which time we'll have no money left anyway.'

'And be too old and knackered.'

'Still, it's good to give things a try.'

'Mmm, though next time when the brochure says "Children's Play Area", it would be useful to find out if there's anything more than one swing.'

From no excitement on holiday, we return to plenty. And it's all going on outside our house. First we have children chucking silver packets into the front garden – something clearly more mood-enhancing than chewing gum. When I go out to remonstrate, they sneer at me. Then a police car hits another car just outside. Then we have to evacuate when – this is shortly after the Brixton and Soho bombings – a suspect package is found on our wall (it turns out to contain stolen car radios). Then one

Sunday morning at 5 a.m. I get up to feed Lydia and see a man in the back garden, making for the house. When he sees me he runs off, but I am shaking. That's followed by a 'joy-riding' incident in which thieves in a stolen red car drive into our car with such force that they push it part-way through our neighbour's front garden. The back axle is nearly off, and we almost lose it altogether. In the space of a few weeks, we dial 999 four times, the fourth one being caused by a cat knocking over a log outside the back door. I don't want to go to sleep at night in case I have to get up and defend my family.

'Most of it's kids from the hostel,' says one of the policemen we are now seeing regularly.

'Hostel . . .?'

'Yeah. But you'll find the problem's mostly at weekends. Sunday nights they usually go back in.'

We decide to sell. A week before her first birthday, Lydia is making her way methodically up the stairs. Unfortunately, I am in the kitchen thinking Peter is minding her, and he is in the sitting room thinking the same. We both hear the dreadful sound of her tumbling down, down, down to the tiles. He reaches her first and picks her up. She is all stiff, and apparently unconscious.

'Omigod! What shall we do? *What shall we do???!!!*'

'She's coming round!'

She opens her eyes, takes a deep breath and cries –

those long, desperate cries that make you want to rip
your guts out and hurl them into the street. I can see
now why the Japanese invented *hara-kiri*. When you feel
this bad, eviscerating yourself can only brighten your
day.

After this first weird fainting fit, she has several more.
The doctor offers me a referral to a paediatrician some
time hence.

'When would that be?'

'Ooh, six to eight weeks. They'll write to you.'

'I'd really like to see someone a bit sooner. I want to
know what it is.'

'Well, I shouldn't think it's epilepsy.'

'Yes, but we don't know. What about Great Ormond
Street? Could I take her there?'

'Ooh, no. Tertiary referrals only.'

'What about private? Peter's got insurance from
work.'

'Oh, we don't want to get into all that, do we?'

Somehow, I find myself leaving with nothing except
this vague offer of an appointment sometime in the next
decade. But when I get home, I ring Liz and Andrew, the
other parents who use Maureen, and both – though not
in our area – GPs.

'Of course you can go to Great Ormond Street,' says Andrew. 'You just ring up their private bit, and get the name of a paediatrician. Then go back – to another GP this time – and ask for a referral letter.'

'And—?'

'That's it. They should see Lydia in two or three days.'

Three days later we are sitting in a private consulting room, with a Dr Shaw. Lydia plays with the toys.

'Sorry she isn't fainting for you,' I say.

'That's all right. Can you describe what happens?'

'If she cries very hard, or falls down and bangs her head – she shuts her eyes and goes stiff. Then she flops, sort of faints. Then she wakes up and continues crying, as if it hadn't happened.'

'And how long is she out for?'

'Not long. Twenty seconds? Less maybe. It's all because she fell down the stairs when we weren't looking. I just feel so terrible.'

'Don't worry,' he says. 'I can tell you exactly what that is. 'They're called Reflex Anoxic Seizures.'

The relief is incredible. Although he's sure it's that and not epilepsy, he books an EEG, and gives me the name of a support group. The EEG is normal, the woman who runs the support group (called Stars) is fantastic, and although Lydia goes on fainting on and off for the next three years or so, it does nothing to hinder her ambition to climb trees, balance on the tops of bunk beds and hurl herself off the climbing frame. But I continue to feel guilty and always feel I have to 'confess' about the stairs.

Our house is on the market. Although I focus on the big garden, rather than the Johannesburg-style crime levels, no one wants to buy it. Also, we don't agree about where we should go. I think we should stay north, where our friends are, and Peter thinks we should go south, where we can still have a garden and be near his sister. I stand firm until we have coffee with a friend of his from work who lives in Dulwich. We see the park, the trees and ooh, a *pergola*. I concede I just might consider moving there. But it will mean leaving Maureen, which is unimaginable. Jump-started into planning by the thought of looking after them myself full-time – a prospect too terrifying to contemplate – I start ringing nurseries in the area. None takes kids in nappies. I get frantic, and snap at Lawrence more than usual.

'You're bad,' he tells me.

I get worse. I switch *Thomas the Tank Engine* off for dinner, and he screams for twenty minutes. We get a temporary respite when we manage to get some food into him, but then Peter accidentally turns to answer the phone at the moment Lawrence offers him a biscuit, and the tantrum resumes. Sharon is there to babysit, and even her magic touch is neutralized. She takes him upstairs to get undressed and he kicks her. Having shouted at him plenty, I remain in the kitchen, trembling with frustration and rage. A few nights later, I make Lydia cry by washing her hair, and he tells me off for that, too.

Still no interest in the house. Sharon tells us she's got a full-time nannying job. As Maureen never works after 5.30, and Sharon is the only other person the children know, our babysitting has just gone up the spout. The main purpose of going out in the evenings is so we can go to the cinema, and Peter can't see a film that starts after seven because he can't stay awake. This has nothing to do with having children; he's always been like that. When we first met, he quickly became known amongst my friends – in a rather Native American sounding way – as *The One Who Falls Asleep*. Many dinner parties have ground to a halt while I, then the host and finally all the other guests stop talking to observe him nodding forward with his mouth open like one of those dogs people used to put in the backs of cars. It's a 6.30 movie or nothing, therefore, and Sharon's new job doesn't finish till half-seven. I can feel myself starting to panic.

'I might be able to get to you around eight,' she says, ruminatively. 'But then again, I might be too tired.' She's looking at an eleven-hour day, which even at her age I'd say is pushing it. Honestly! These middle-class types have no consideration. I plunge into gloom until she reveals that though the mother works long hours in a bank or somewhere, the father of the children in question works at home.

'What?! So what's with the 7.30? He can stop any-time!' I work at home and I'll stop for anything: to gaze at the cloud formations, straighten my paper-clips or fall into a happy trance picking my nose.

'Yeah, but he don't,' Sharon points out.

'Yes, but he could.'

'But he don't.'

This is getting us nowhere. I decide to go and talk to him. We have mutual friends; it'll be fine.

'Are you sure this is a good idea?' says Peter.

'I'm only going to ask.'

I get there, and the conversation goes like this:

'I was wondering if you would consider releasing Sharon an hour early on some days.'

'No. You see, she replaces my wife, not me.'

'I'm sorry? I don't quite—'

'I don't look after the children, my wife does.'

'So – um . . .'

'Sorry, no can do. Sharon will be here until 7.30, when she comes home.'

Even though I've got nowhere, we part on friendly terms. I get home and the phone rings. It is Sharon. She says: 'I'm really angry that you spoke to him when I asked you not to!' She puts the phone down and that is that.

'We've got no one now. We'll never go out again!'

'We can stay in,' he says. 'You can cook.'

'Oh, cheers.'

'You love cooking.' This is true, but I'm hoping he's forgotten.

'I'm trapped! Help! Help!'

'We'll find another babysitter.'

'Where???!'

'You found Sharon. You'll find someone else.'

'I won't. I won't!' I yank the cork out of a bottle. 'And we're stuck in this scary house. We'll probably all be killed.'

'No, we won't. We're going to move to Dulwich and then we'll be too far away for Sharon anyway.'

'I'm not moving to fucking south London. You bastard! First you charm me into getting married! Then you trick me into getting a mortgage. *Then* you make me have *children*. *Now* you're trying to force me to live – *Down There*.'

'You left Bloomsbury.'

'More fool me.'

'We can have a big garden. It'll be nice.'

'Yeah, in SE *300*.'

'My sister lives there. You like her.'

'What about *my* friends? I can't walk to Soho. There's not even a tube. I'll never see Claire or Tilly or Claudia again. My life is ruined. I hate you!'

'It'll be fine.'

'Yeah. Well, you know what? We don't need a babysitter now anyway, because I'm leaving.'

'There, you see? Problem solved.'

12 To A&E by Double Buggy

Finally we have a firm offer on the house. Desperate not to lose the buyer, I exchange contracts. We haven't found anywhere else to live.

Peter says: 'I trust you completely.'

'Well, at least that way you'll always have someone to blame.'

Weeks go by. Every Monday and Tuesday I ring fifty estate agents. Everything is too big and expensive, or too small, or has no garden, or has had all the storage ripped out to install 'en suites'. One has been *feng shui'd* and had the front door turned eleven degrees to the left, or the south, or towards Shanghai, but anyhow it doesn't matter because it's hideous and reeks of dogs.

'That's it,' I tell Peter finally. 'There are no four-bedroomed houses with gardens in south London. There just aren't.'

Then, when we are about to become homeless, a house pops up in the same road as our friend with the pergola. It's long and thin, like our first house turned on its side. When we go to look round, there is a teenager on the sofa reading the *Financial Times*.

'I've seen show flats where they put a plastic croissant on the table, but nothing like this.'

The children love it.

'There's even a shed, so they can have a den.'

'Somewhere to smoke!'

And so we leave the bars and shops of Islington, north London, for the tree-lined avenues of Dulwich in the south. I have been assuming that Lawrence and Lydia will be traumatized by losing Maureen. She's a nurturing and observant carer of children, but by the time we've booked the moving lorry, I've turned her into a cross between Mary Poppins and Melanie Klein. In fact they turn out to be quite unbothered, whereas I have been crying on and off since we exchanged contracts eight weeks ago. The thought of managing without her quiet, clean house to leave them in, the idea of losing the routine – this crutch – fills me with panic. I am going to be alone with them both for the first time, nowhere near my friends, and am trembling with chronic, low-level dread.

On moving day, we take Lawrence to Maureen's as usual, so we can finish packing. At 1 p.m., with the lorry on its way, we go to fetch him. In accordance with Maureen's routine, they have already begun their daily visit to the One O'Clock Club. This is Lynn's domain. She manages it, and apart from a press release I did for the local papers when it was threatened with closure, we have had no contact.

When we arrive and see the breadth of activities laid on, I feel a surge of guilt. *Two* other people have been educating my child – stimulating him, widening his skill base and doing all the stuff I should be doing. His passably good manners are surely down to Maureen. She doesn't swear, which gives her a head start over me. And she handles all those tricky management issues, like toy sharing. But I've assumed that the stunning splashes of colour Lawrence brings home are due to my fabulously artistic DNA.

Wrong! All the kids here are geniuses. The walls are bedecked with a dazzling display of infant talent. The Wendy house is stocked with dressing-up clothes, there are pots of paint, glitter, things to stick, plus books, and even a little reading corner with a sofa. We'd been worrying about the standard of Islington's schools: no need! He could have spent the next eight years here.

We say hello – and goodbye – to the Incredible Lynn. Maureen hugs Lawrence and tells us: 'The plaster on his forehead is because he had a little fall on the sofa.' She gestures at the reading area. The sofa is made of wood. 'He's got a little cut, but he's fine. Aren't you, Lawrence?' And indeed, he is not bothered at all.

'Goodbye, good luck!'

'Goodbye. Thanks for everything!'

'Bye!'

'Wave bye-bye, Lawrence!'

'Bye-bye . . .'

We load him into the car, repack Lydia, and head south.

At the other end, Peter wants to put away his precious 1960s pedal car, so he carries it through the house to the garden, to take to the shed. But as he holds it over the back doorstep, he gives a cry and drops to the floor.

'What?! What is it?!'

'My back!'

He can't move. I feed some aspirin into his mouth and pour water over his face to swallow them with.

'Ow!' (Splash.) '*Ow!*'

I can do nothing but leave him lying there, with the removal men stepping over him. Once the table's unloaded, I attach Lawrence and Lydia to it in their escape-proof screw-on chairs. Lawrence's cut, much nearer his eye than I'd realized, is looking slightly inflamed. Should I be worried? The men finish and go away, leaving us with our boxes and Peter, like a draught excluder, along the back door. I leave the children at the table, so they can occupy themselves gouging out the varnish with their spoons while I get on the phone to try and find someone to look at Peter's back.

We ring the vendor, who is an anaesthetist. Apparently one of our new neighbours is a physio, two doors along. What a useful street we've moved into! She comes round and bends over the prostrate husband. She is cheery in blue eye-shadow.

'Ooh, dear! What have you done there?'

'Nnnhhh.'

'Stay still, keep taking the anti-inflammatries, and try not to *sit*.'

'Not much danger of that.'

It's one way to meet the neighbours.

When she's gone he turns sideways and says: 'Can you bring me a saucepan?'

'Er, why?'

'I need something to pee into.'

The next day, one side of Lawrence's forehead is still red, and looking distinctly bigger than the other. We get a call from Katarina, who's been looking after Mira's children, and might be available two days a week. She's been to see us a couple of times at the old house, and clearly adores kids. I have no idea how to interview people – *'Er, are you nice or horrible?'* – so am hoping my first impression, that she's a natural, will be right. Meanwhile, there's a surgery within walking distance, so I get out the double buggy and wheel the kids round. The receptionist is friendly and concerned. She can't have been to medical receptionist training school.

'It's infected,' says the doctor. 'I'm going to prescribe antibiotics, I'm afraid.'

Afraid? Ah, yes: she's anticipating automatic middle-class resistance.

'No, no: please. Stuff them in.'

Great service! We haven't even registered yet.

Back home, Peter is only just beginning to crawl. I suddenly feel less guilty about getting some help, so ring back Katarina.

'I can come on Friday,' she says. 'But only for the morning. I have another job in the afternoon.'

'Whatever! Anything would be great.'

Two days later, the side of Lawrence's head is even redder, and bigger. The doctor gazes at him steadily.

'Ah, yes . . .'

'What?'

'The oral antibiotics don't seem to have worked.'

'And therefore . . .?'

Her hand is on the phone.

'Paediatric Admissions, please. No, I'll hold.' She

suddenly hands me the phone. 'I'll be back in a sec. If anyone answers, you're holding for Dr Waitt.'

'Er, OK . . .'

She returns with a piece of paper.

'This is what he's been taking. Just show them this when you get there. D'you know where King's is? A&E Department. Just walk round. They're expecting you.'

'Er, OK. What he has got?'

'Cellulitis.'

'What's the worst-case scenario? I promise not to panic.'

'When it's in the head like this . . . Meningitis.'

'Lawrence, back in the buggy. *Now!*'

On the way up the hill, I review the events that have brought us to this. Let's see . . . I had children – probably a mistake, as I didn't want to look after them full-time like Proper Mothers. So I took Lawrence to Maureen's. And that was mainly so I could have some time to myself, and do some work – according to research always being quoted in the newspapers, a Bad Thing. Then, while in the care of Maureen – with whom I had a financial arrangement, so it's not like she was my mother or something which would have been morally justifiable – he fell over and got a bad cut. Now the cut is infected, his head is blowing up like a tomato, and he might die. So clearly, this is all my fault.

172

The A&E Department is populated by those old, drunk men who seem to do nothing but fall over and go to A&E Departments. The admissions staff, I am amazed to discover, are more interested in finding Lawrence a bed than criticizing me. He has to have a line into his hand and be given intravenous antibiotics every four hours. My little boy! OK, *think*. I queue for the payphone, with Lawrence all needled up like a dwarf junkie and Lydia squirming in the buggy. She's still here with us; Peter can barely lift a newspaper, let alone her. How am I going to do this?

'We're at King's.'

'Oh, my God . . .'

'He's going to be all right, but—'

'I want to go to the playroom.'

'In a minute. He's got to have intravenous antibiotics every four hours and stay at least two nights.'

'I want to go to the playroom.'

'Can you ring Katarina? And maybe get her to meet me here?'

'Mum-meee!!!'

'OK. I'll try and—'

'Playroom! *PLAYROOM!!!!!*'

'In a MINUTE! I'm not raising my voice at you. And can you ring Claire?'

I have no idea if Katarina can rise to the challenge,

but Claire will make everything all right. She has no children, is younger than me and lives in Kent. But in a crisis, she's the one. She came to Australia after our car accident and brought me frozen yogurt.

We go to the playroom. Lawrence gets hold of a toy train and despite the needle in his hand, plays delightedly. I let Lydia out of the buggy, and wait. I don't have nappies, extra milk or a toothbrush. And I forgot to ask Peter about his back. I'm a bad mother *and* wife. At least Claire can't disown me; we're related. Maybe in this situation I can redeem myself, be *marvellous*. Yeah, that's a good idea. I'll sleep on the floor – judging by the look of that ward I'm going to have to – and not have a shower or anything, and perhaps that will make up for it. Lawrence isn't going to die, anyhow. *He is going to be fine.*

The children are running towards the door. Well, Lawrence is. Lydia is shuffling.

'Katarina! Katarina!'

She picks them up and hugs them. And she has a carrier bag in one hand.

'Hello! I thought you might need some nappies.'

'!'

She takes Lydia home in the buggy, and Claire arrives. She's brought a book for Lawrence, and a toothbrush, flannel and soap for me. Plus deodorant.

'In a crisis, it always helps to smell nice.'

'Oh, Claire . . .'

'Hey, it's all right.'

'He's been at Maureen's for ages, and it's all been fine!'

'Of course it has.'

'I didn't know he was going to fall and cut himself.'

'Of course you didn't.'

I slump tearfully into a chair. Lawrence is having a great time. Because he won't leave the toy train, the nurse agrees to give him his meds in the playroom. I sit him on my lap, and she unwraps the end bit of the tape holding the line in place. Suddenly he cries. The nurse is completely unmoved. Claire lifts up the end of the line, which is hanging out over Lawrence's hand, and therefore pulling on the needle.

She says: 'Isn't he crying because this bit should be held up?'

'Oh. Yes . . . Sorry, I'm not very good with needles.'

I'm having a bad feeling about this. This is not like any hospital I've ever been in. It's more like a black-market version of one. Any minute now, we'll see Harry Lime with the drugs trolley. Claire continues to hold the line up until it's done, talking to Lawrence soothingly the while. I tell him how fantastic he's being, which he is.

'Can I play now, Mummy?'

'Yes, darling.'

Four hours later, it's time for the next dose, but there's no sign of the nurse – or anyone. Eventually we find one. She prepares the medicine and gazes vaguely at her watch.

'What time did he have the last lot?'

'Well, about ten past two,' I say.

Claire says: 'Shouldn't she know that? Isn't there a chart where they're supposed to write it down?'

Eventually, we have to put him to bed. But the ward is heaving with children and parents, and the television is blaring. And hang on – is that *another* television beside the bed opposite? There's a teenage boy lying there, not looking ill at all, and he's not even watching it. Two or three grown-ups are watching the main TV. It doesn't look as though we can get it switched off, as it's only eight o'clock, even if it is a children's ward. So I start drawing the curtain round Lawrence's bed to at least block out some of the light, that special, ultra-bright dazzling light that hospitals like to keep on so they can see you while you don't sleep. A voice calls from the desk.

'Can you put it back, please?'

'I'm sorry?'

'You're not allowed to draw the curtains.'

'We're just trying to help my child get some sleep. Why not?'

'We have to be able to see the girl in the bed behind him, and she keeps fitting.'

In the narrow space between beds, as if in a Jacques Tati film, Claire attempts to unfold the chair-bed they provide for parents. She takes that, while I lie down next to Lawrence.

At 11 p.m., both tellies are still going, loudly, and the teenage boy is playing cards with a girl. I've been to nightclubs quieter than this.

'Can you *please* switch off the TVs?'

'All right.'

But they don't. Eventually, we get a few fragments of sleep before Lawrence has to be woken anyway for the next dose. None of the nurses are like nurses, or not like any nurses I've ever met. They're more like schoolkids doing their least favourite lesson. And there is no sign whatsoever of a doctor. Later, I go past the desk to see a nurse sitting beside a large tin of biscuits.

'Could I possibly have one?'

She gestures sullenly at the tin. She has her feet on the desk.

'Claire . . .'

'Mm.'

'Are you asleep?'

'Yes, I always sleep with a poker game and two tellies on.'

'Thanks for coming.'

'Anytime. I like an outing.'

In the morning, Lawrence bounces cheerfully off to the playroom while Claire staggers off to find the coffee machine.

'I can't do another night of *that*,' I say.

'Does he have to actually stay in?'

A doctor appears – like normal hospitals, they do actually have ward rounds – and I turn into Hattie Jacques.

'We've had a *dreadful* night,' I tell him, 'with *two* televisions on, which they refused to turn off, and that boy over there playing cards till God knows when. And they wouldn't even let us draw the curtains! How can you expect patients to get better like this?'

'Well . . .' I wait for the apology, or the explanation, or *something*. None is forthcoming. He doesn't care.

'Right!' Something unusual is happening. I hear a voice saying, 'I'm taking him home. He doesn't have to actually stay here, right?' The voice is *mine*.

'He has to have the antibiotics every four hours.'

'So I'll set the alarm and bring him back. OK?'

The guy is clearly relieved to get rid of us.

Claire is impressed.

'Ooh, well done!'

I feel weird and very slightly high, as if I've just been

178

to a foreign country and been magically able to speak the language.

Claire and I take Lawrence back at four, eight and midnight and, as he can now move about, Peter and I do 4 a.m. His head has gone down, and is almost back to normal. He's sorry to leave because he misses the playroom. The needle is finally gone, but he keeps the little plastic bracelet. I don't believe in telling children to be brave, but then with him I haven't needed to. What other amazing qualities will he reveal to us in the coming years? I speculate about this, proudly, as I fall asleep in my own bed.

13 Oi-U and Non Oi-U

Alone with them all day, I am shattered. Katarina now comes for half a day on a Tuesday and a Friday, but on the other days, by 3 p.m. I'm often crashing out for seconds at a time, with the two of them crawling over me. Trying to get them to have their nap at the same time is like trying to do those impossible games with the little silver balls; as one goes in, the other rolls out. And now, at two and a half, Lawrence is giving his up. I complain to Peter: 'Having them so close together was your idea.'

'It'll be fine.'

'Really? You want to come home and do this?'

I start looking forward to Katarina's two half-days like a POW awaiting the Red Cross. In between we watch a lot of videos, whose volume I keep turning down to the level where I can tune out and grab a few minutes' sleep. And I quickly start 'losing' the most irritating ones, e.g. *Bob*

the Builder and the not surprisingly less famous *Titch* –
dramatic theme: he is smaller than his siblings. Subversive subtext: none. Some armies play music to get them
in the killing mood; well, *Titch* does it for me. I prefer
Thomas the Tank Engine (& Friends), with its explosions,
crashes and trains falling off bridges. *Pingu*'s morose
Scandinavian humour appeals, too, along with the behaviour of his parents: irritable dad and anxious mum, who
in one episode go away for the weekend, leaving Pingu
and the baby *alone in the house* with nothing to eat but
popcorn. We've got the bumper edition which has about
500 episodes on it. But for post-modern subtext we like
Fireman Sam, a Welsh bachelor unable to form bonds
with adults who lives in a village where two sex-starved,
post-menopausal women compete for the attentions of a
dyspraxic bus driver. There's very little action; Excitable
Italian Bella Lasagne has to set fire to her cafe every
week so they can get out the fire engine.

Apart from that we have one other activity, which is
playing with the toy garage. We push the cars down the
slope, and sometimes, for variety, jam them in the lift.
Then I unjam them, while working out exactly how long
it is until they can both start some kind of full-time
education. Two years. I'm not sure I can make it that far.

*

I take a deep breath and tackle nurseries. After a mixture of phoning and SAS-style swoops, I finally discover three in the immediate area that take children in nappies. All the others require them to be dry by two and a half, which is a clever trick, says my mother, since their bottoms and other bits only start getting under their control at about that age. The posh mummies' venue of choice is a well-appointed house with garden, and positively swarming with nursery assistants. Round here it's clearly regarded as the Savoy of nurseries. It even takes babies. But the rows of sleeping mats, and the girls in plastic gloves changing nappies, puts me in mind of orphanages I've seen on the news, and despite the lovely building and great word of mouth, I can't face it.

The second one is in a cavernous church hall, and is Montessori. I have a reflexive aversion to the M-word, having done time at a weird Montessori primary school. But I overcome it and take Lawrence to see the Head, who sits down with him and gets out some of the superb wooden learning aids, such as beautifully turned cylinders with lids in ascending size. She gently encourages him to line them up in order, and he clearly enjoys himself. We go away happy, and I am in the process of weighing up the long walk, versus the wonderful Head versus the slightly gloomy church building, when it burns down.

That leaves Treetops, also in a church but a cheerier one, and only a short buggy-push away. The staff are seemingly more qualified in playing in the Wendy house than actual teaching skills. But Lawrence is two, not twelve, and I want him just to get out of the house for a few hours and have a nice time, not start his GCSEs.

On the day he's supposed to start there, he refuses to leave without his toy supermarket trolley. We line up to cross the road, and as I bend down to do up Lydia's shoe I realize he isn't holding my hand. When I look up again he is in the middle of the road with his trolley, and there is a car in front of him. It seems to have stopped, but the scene looks like a freeze-frame. When I dash out – will it rev up again and run him down? – I grab him, and the wretched trolley, but feel so sick we have to turn back. I ring Treetops and ask if he can start the next day instead, but don't think I can ever take them out of the house again.

'Jesus,' says Peter. 'Still, these things happen.'

'No, I can't do this. We'll just have to move to New Zealand.'

The next day, Lydia takes her first step.

'You clever girl!' says Peter.

'Bit of a waste, as I'm never letting them out again.'

I do take Lawrence to Treetops, hang around for the first couple of days, and drift off home for another day of jamming cars in the toy garage and watching *Fireman Sam*.

Very quickly, the route to nursery becomes boring. As my interest in cars has increased under Peter's influence, I start teaching Lawrence how to recognize them by their badges. It alleviates the monotony of passing the same takeaway, newsagent and dry cleaner's, and will be a useful grounding should he follow the Calman tradition and go into design.

'What's the blue oval?'

'Ford.' And so on. Lions quickly become 'Peugeots'. And within weeks he is identifying a Metro, which has no distinguishing features, and – spooky, this – a Vauxhall *with no badge*. But as usual, we have succumbed to Short Termism.

'Lawrence, look up at the lovely pink sky!'

'Vauxhall!'

Still, to look on the bright side, Lydia is now pushing the double buggy. The time when we can rid ourselves of the beastly vehicle is in sight. As Shea, my old nanny, always says: *One door closes: another door opens.* You just have to make sure a child isn't standing on the other side.

Although Treetops doesn't mind nappies, Katarina is encouraging us to give them up.

'But nappies are so convenient, so easy!'

'Yes, but he needs to learn to use the toilet.'

I tell her about the perverse couplings with Champagne doll and the Playmobil pilot.

'I'm no good at this. Honestly.'

'I'll help you, don't worry.'

In the end she pretty much does the whole thing. I am not shirking; I'm learning to delegate. Anyhow, the job needs someone with a combination of attributes that I don't possess, i.e. patience and persistence. Somewhere in the back of my mind a voice says: *You're going to become dependent on her.* But I shove it away. After all, I'm dependent on Peter. You can't spend your whole life avoiding anyone useful in case they leave. I mean, John Lewis used to do this wonderful mascara for £1.95, then suddenly they stopped. I pleaded with the cosmetics buyer, but eventually I got on with my life. One does.

Anyhow, I've got more important things on my mind. Are we going to keep Lawrence at Treetops until primary school, or take the advice of someone we don't know very well – admittedly an expert in these matters, well OK, a teacher – who's begging us to see the local prep school? We weigh up the pros and cons.

'OK: pro.'

'Small classes. Plenty of sport.'

'Expensive. And plenty of sport.'

'Rich peer group. Might take him on good holidays.'

'Rich peer group. All his friends will have their own villas in Mustique.'

'Well, if you're going to be silly.'

'Excuse me! Your friend John's girls go to a school where fourteen year olds have their own cars and *drivers*.'

'That's a total one-off.'

'No it isn't: the chauffeurs all drive them to their second houses in Rock. You just don't like state schools because the one you went to was full of skinheads.'

'And *you* don't like private schools because the one *you* went to was run by a nutter.'

'So?'

'So?'

'Copycat.'

'*Nyer!*'

Out of curiosity we phone anyway. The Head is charming.

'And how old is Lawrence?'

'Two.'

'We normally hear from people a little earlier than this' (i.e. before conception).

'Ah, well, you see, we've just moved. From *Islington*,' I add, going for the sympathy vote. Mrs Adams said we should call.'

'Mrs Adams! Oh, I know her work well!'

We barely know Mrs Adams. We know her son, sort of. But she teaches the older boys, and her name clearly opens doors.

'Bring him along next week.'

The nursery department is in a rather style-free prefab, but with slides and other outdoor kit, a big grass field to play in, and flower beds. A dinner lady brings us some coffee and we look at the children's work on the walls.

'So what d'you think?'

'Mmm. Good biscuits.'

Lawrence is clutching the favourite toy he's been asked to bring, a crane he and Peter have made out of Duplo. This is where having a child who won't shut up comes into its own. He chats to any adult who stands still long enough, or who can't get away. One day I leave him outside Oddbins – he stops there automatically now – and find him delivering some kind of talk to a woman in a wheelchair. I don't know whether she's charmed, or has just lost the will to push herself away. Anyhow, it's just the sort of thing to get him through the selection process. The only problem is getting him to stop. The Head takes him away to talk about his crane, and when they return, he's still babbling behind her.

'He's had a lovely time.'

'Oh, good. Er, is that it?'

'We'll write to you by the end of next week.'

'So what d'you think?'

'The teachers are very nicely dressed,' says Peter.

'Oh, well that settles it.'

Meanwhile we carry on at Treetops. Then I come in one day to get Lawrence, with Lydia as usual, and a small boy approaches.

'Baby!' he says. 'Baby!'

'That's right . . .' I say. He grabs her leg and starts to pull.

'Baby!'

I'm crouching with her on my lap. He pulls harder and she starts to slide off. I growl at him: *'Get off!'* He doesn't. We tussle until I wobble backwards and we all end up on the floor.

'Don't do that, Jason,' says one of the girls.

Whenever I come in after this I hold Lydia up, like a rifle in a swamp. But Jason isn't the only problem. There is also Maurice, as strong as Jason, but even more unpredictable, a sort of Charles Bronson character in shorts. He scares *me*.

When I ask Lawrence: 'How was nursery today?' he says: 'I don't like Maurice.'

'Did you play in the kitchen corner? Did you build a—'

'I don't like Maurice, Mummy.'

I like Treetops because the staff are laid-back, and you can pick your own hours. Plus they serve fruit at break-time and it's only £20 a day. On the other hand, if your child's too scared to go, it's not such a bargain. Luckily, we can avoid a decision by awaiting the letter from the prep school. When it arrives with a yes, we are all relieved. We have made the right choice. Probably. We think. Definitely. Probably.

14 Sex with Thomas the Tank Engine (& Friends)

Sitting on the downstairs loo in our new house, I browse the pinboard. Amongst the curry menus, next to an ad from someone called Krysta offering *'cleaning and irony'*, a newspaper cutting catches my eye. It's a cartoon I once cut out of the *New Yorker*, showing a sensible-looking couple sitting in armchairs.

'Now the kids have grown and gone,' says the man, *'I thought it might be a good time for us to have sex.'*

And I realize it's not as funny as it was before.

I treasure the *memory* of sex, but it feels like too much effort – like hearing there's free money being given away in Oxford Street, but it's rush hour and you have to get on the tube. Anyhow, what I really fantasize about is sleep. Toddlers need at least ten hours, say the books, and I need eight. Sex? This tired, I wouldn't cross the room for George Clooney. After several days on less than four hours a night, I change personality. It starts with wanting to kill people over parking spaces, and attacking

Peter over his nose hair. Then within a fortnight I'm signing up for cults with smiley people at stations and saying we should make a move to Devon and create a sustainable community built entirely from peat. Why is sleep deprivation used by despots around the world as a torture? Because it *is* one. So why the fuck should we worry about *sex*? It's just one more thing TO DO, one more thing on the Giant List of Life:

Meet non-useless, non-psychopathic man.

Have children.

Try to restart career.

Go to a film/play/gallery/somewhere that's open after
   6 p.m.

Read a book that doesn't have the words 'Little',
   'Hugs' or 'Bear' in the title.

Have an uninterrupted conversation.

You see? I didn't even intend to leave it out. And – be honest – did you notice? The trouble is, it's so – expendable. I like it, but it's amazing how easy it is to do without it. Wine I can't live without. Or meat. But sex . . . I've never heard anyone on *Desert Island Discs* ask Sue Lawley for a vibrator.

My mother's generation were of the view that if anything went wrong in a marriage, it would invariably be because *He wasn't happy in bed*. Which was always *Her Fault*. And we know the medical profession still think that way because of the speed with which they send round the thin young nurses with the contraception leaflets. Think: what do women most want after they've given birth? If you answered *'Penetrative Sex'* you are either (a) a doctor, or (b) a (very stupid) man.

This idea, that men go to pieces if they have to do without it for two minutes is bollocks. We go without chocolate – sometimes for days. And even if it isn't bollocks, no new mother has it as her top priority. All you want is sleep. And once a man is as deprived of it as you are, he won't remember what sex is either. He'll either want to rest, or die.

Nearly two years after having Lydia, we are at the epicentre of toddler-induced exhaustion. The books acknowledge that babies make you tired, but babies can be put in slings and walked about, or driven around, or knocked out with nipples. A two and a three year old just crush you with an energy that makes nuclear power look feeble. Steven Spielberg's first film, *Duel*, has a man being pursued by a seemingly driverless lorry. Wherever he tries to go, it follows him, bearing down on him in a terrifying way. It's clearly a metaphor for life with the under-fives, and in the path of it, who thinks about sex?

The writers of books on the subject generally recommend you talk about it. I've never met anyone who wanted to do that. (Well, not to their man anyway.) The experts think we should all be 'open' about it. They love the word 'open', which is probably why no woman I've ever met takes their advice. Another word they love is 'initiate'.

'I'd like to initiate sex,' says Peter, if he wants to creep me out. He did try to inject it with a bit more allure, once: tried the Warren Beatty tactic. At about 8.30 he rang me up and said, 'I'm ten minutes away. Take off your pants.' But his train got stuck outside London Bridge, so I put on my thick socks and ate a whole trifle for four.

I've got a book from the eighties that advises you not to criticize while on the job – i.e. don't say: '*You are total crap*' while they're actually Doing It – but wait until you're dressed and then say: '*I'd like to make some time to talk about sex.*' This puts me in mind of applying at some kind of desk.

As for magazine articles, like '*Put the spice back into your sex life*', they make me want to refuse to do it ever again. What do you mean? Pepper? And they're very keen on lacy underwear. Well, when Ann Summers starts a section called 'Post-Partum Party' they'll know there's a demand for it.

Still, I do miss it. Not as much as an amazing orange-flavoured bread and butter pudding I had in 1992 in Bristol, which I still think about. But quite a bit. And I'm just slightly concerned that Peter has started to refer to it with the same nostalgic fondness he used to reserve for flying boats and the Age of Steam. He hasn't actually complained, but I think he's relegated it to our Former Life, along with reading a whole section of the Sunday newspapers and talking without interruptions on the phone. I make a decision. I'm going to Consider His Needs. I won't change my pants, as it were, but I will *initiate*. I picture him at work. I've always found offices quite sexy. I had sex with a guy on his desk once. Apart from a sore back because of the stapler, it was quite good. Mind you, these days the arousal threshold is lower. When your life is dominated by two year olds, just being near a man in a suit is quite thrilling. And the phrase *'Let's do lunch'* is practically foreplay. Right! I'm focused now. I'll ring up and get him in the mood. *Pip-pip-pip-pip* (that's me dialling).

'Hi ... I just thought you should know, that – I'd really like to fuck you sometime.'

'Actually, can I call you back? I'm in a meeting.'

And by the time he does get home all we want to do is eat, drink and go to sleep. That leaves early morning –

the only part of the day where energy and quiet are available at the same time, except that at the moment the kids wake nearly every day at five. A few days later, however, we get our chance. It's 6.30 and they're still asleep.

'Shall we?'

'Yeah, go on.'

'What if they wake up?'

'They're very quiet.'

'D'you think something's wrong?'

'We should check on them.'

'Yeah, but that'll wake them up. It did last time.'

'OK, go on.'

'I think I heard something.'

'No, no. Hurry up, they're fine.'

Sex! Quick, quick, boy! An ecstasy of fumbling. I pull off the non-lacy pants and hurl them across the room. But it's harder to throw off the guilt. I remember when my friend Claudia unplugged the baby monitor to put in a cappuccino machine. As we drank we made up head-lines: '*Tragic Tots Died So Parents Could Have Frothy Coffee.*' Some bit of me is absolutely convinced that if I let them go out of my head, even for a minute, something bad will happen. Still, I've got the pants off now. Fifteen minutes in, when we've forgotten that we even *have* any children:

'Da-a-a-a-d-e-e-eee!!!'

We stop dead, look guiltily at the door.

'Maybe they'll go back to sleep.'

'D-A-A-A-*DDE-E-E-E-EEEEE!!!*'

'Coming!' Ha, bloody, ha.

We go into their room. Lawrence is halfway over the bars of his cot with an expression of pained self-righteousness, like Jack Klugman in *Twelve Angry Men*. Lydia is rattling hers and shouting incoherent abuse, like the alcoholic prostitute in the flats near where I used to live. Peter has a brainwave.

'Hey, what about a video?'

'Thanks, but if I can't have sex myself, the last thing I want to see is someone else having it.'

'Not you: *them.*'

'Yes, *please*!!' says Lawrence.

'Minamin!' This is Lydia's name for Thomas the Tank Engine. I don't know why.

'Right! Where is it?'

'Downstairs.'

'Come on everyone! Quick!'

A straggly procession makes its way downstairs, taking ages because Lawrence has to stop for a wee, which he's just learned how to do, and Lydia gets halfway then has to go back for her favourite purple scarf.

'Sit down, everyone. Not there!'

Lawrence has sat on my non-removable-covered little

armchair, the only one in the house I mind about, and since starting toilet training, his favourite. Peter holds up *Thomas The Tank Engine & Friends*, which is only fifteen minutes: not long enough. Well, not for me anyway.

'Get *Rescues on the Railways*. That's the longest.'

It's thirty-four minutes – long enough even for me. But we can't find it. We search frantically, chucking tapes all over the place.

'Don't throw things,' says Lawrence. 'You're very *naughty*.'

We have three episodes of *Homicide*, two copies of *Saving Private Ryan* – why do people keep giving us that? – a selection of documentaries about penguins and other marine life and one about women's rights in Afghanistan – a very short one, ha-ha. *Rescues on the Railways* remains elusive.

'Hey, look: *The Big Sleep*!'

'*Great*. I thought it'd gone forever.'

'You said I never packed it when we moved. I did. *See?* And you didn't believe me, you said—'

'Wait, what's this?'

It's *Spooks and Surprises* – late period Thomas with ghost trains, crashes and explosions, with beautiful special effects. And it's a whopping fifty-three minutes long.

'I love this!' shouts Lawrence.

'Minamin!' cries Lydia.

'Oh, look – it's the one with the boulder!'

'OK, they're hooked. Let's go.'

'It's rolling along the track – like *Raiders of the Lost Ark*!'

'Darling . . .'

'Look, look: it's going to explode!'

'Oh *ye-eah* . . .'

We both know the moment has passed. Well, I don't know about you, but I find the switching back and forth a challenge. When you're meant to be Nurturing all the time, you can't just suddenly reboot. If you're still feeding, it's too weird; it's not as though your breasts get new software. And the brain needs time. It's harder than decimals when new pence came in, and that took five years.

But we don't give up. That evening we find *Rescues on the Railways* behind some poster paints and instead of dinner, rush upstairs. In the afterglow, we smile dreamily at each other.

'Darling?'

'Mmm.'

'How long d'you think before they'll want to see *Saving Private Ryan*?'

So, if you thought sex was a thing of the past, like reading the papers properly, here's my Handy Table of

Sexual Activities for some of the videos you're already likely to have around the house (NB TV series are per episode unless otherwise stated):

> *Pingu* – A snog, or, if from the UK, parts of Northern Europe or Australia, foreplay.
>
> *Fireman Sam*, *Balamory*, *The Tweenies* – Oral sex (for him) or, if from the UK, parts of Northern Europe or Australia, full sex.
>
> *Dumbo*, *Mary Poppins*, etc. – Oral sex (for her), full sex and cigarette.
>
> *Lord of the Rings Parts I, II* and *III* – I think I've made my point.

Sex is just the beginning. A whole vista of possibilities has opened up. Soon, we will be able to do something we've *really* missed, like sleep in till eight o'clock.

15 The Worst Mother in the World

September comes. Lawrence has already been to nursery, so it's not as though this is a challenge. We won't have any hysterics, like you get with these boys who've never been away from their mums. You know the ones: their hair's always too long and for some reason they wear dungarees. There's only one teensy problem. He hasn't been to the school since July, six weeks ago. I say, 'You're going to school!' And he says, 'I've *been* to school,' as if it's a one-off, like going to the opera.

He's unbothered, but I feel immediately that I don't fit in and no one will want to be my friend. Thank God I've brought Katarina.

The other mummies seem to fall into two groups. They're either dressed for takeover bids and leaving their child with a guilt-free peck on the forehead before departing for the City by helicopter, or they're coolly shepherding hordes of dogs and older children back into their UN-issue, All-Terrain Personnel Carriers while memorizing the contents of the notice board. Even a child mislaid, or found in the woods with its head down a badger hole, doesn't faze them.

'Come *out*, William . . .' is the most stressed response I hear. None of them looks weepy, or even nervous. Some of them even roll their eyes at each other and exchange knowing looks. What *is* that Look? What are we *doing* here?

On the way in, the children are to have their pictures taken with their mummies. But at the crucial moment Lydia tries to escape, and as I grab her, the teacher leaps forward and photographs Lawrence with Katarina by mistake. There is now incontrovertible evidence that I Have Help. But as Peter always says when I moan about something trivial, 'What you need is a Bigger Problem.' And I soon get one.

Today is just the first day of a two-week settling-in period, with the new children left for an hour the first time, and then longer each day. An hour, or even two, is hardly enough time to do anything. As a result, for days on end the village is full of women wandering around looking at their watches every two minutes and saying, '*I must get back to the South Circular*,' like Robert Shaw in *The Caretaker*.

'Is this really necessary?' I say to the teacher. 'Lawrence has been to nursery before. In fact, we've moved house, *and* he went to hospital. He can cope with anything!'

And sure enough, he coasts along perfectly until the first full day, when I kiss him and walk cheerily to the door. He follows me and clings to my legs, shouting. It feels *terrible*. I try to be frightfully British. It feels like *Sophie's Choice* but I'm trying desperately for *Brief Encounter*: '*Separation Anxiety? Nonsense, Dr Freud! I have some shrapnel in my eye.*'

In full view of the Teacher, the Classroom Assistant and the Student, I am crying before I reach the hall. Lawrence follows me; I bring him back. Three times. Finally they peel him off me like leg wax and I stumble away. I'm all the more humiliated because I'm the only one. I tell Mira back in north London. Hers go to a place where they don't even let you in the door; you have to dispatch the child at arm's length, like plutonium. She says: 'He was probably set off by the others crying.'

But, no: it's just me and him. They say he stops soon after I leave, and he does. I know, because I double back through the cloakroom and listen. Even so, at the end of a torturous week, the teacher calls me to one side.

'It might be better if someone else brings him. Katarina perhaps?'

I feel as though I've just been sacked.

In the end we take turns. I'm half relieved to share the burden, and half determined to show I'm not so inadequate I can't take my own child to school. There is one more thing. The teacher mentions that Lawrence has kicked the Head. I ring up, expecting him to be expelled.

'He's done *what*?'

'I am sorry . . .' she begins.

'*You're* sorry?!'

'We had to take him to the staffroom for a little while.'

'How's your *leg*?'

'Oh, I'm fine!'

'I feel terrible.'

'Now, you mustn't. We simply took him aside for a little while, till he calmed down.'

Jesus.

'I'm really sorry. I don't know what to say.'

'Everything's quite all right. It's very nice of you to ring.'

At least I won't have this trouble with Lydia. She can't even talk yet, and she's already trying to sit on the mat with the others. She's like an automatic car; I just have to let my foot off the gas. That night she picks up the ray gun Peter brought me years ago from Tokyo, his idea of a romantic present. She waves it and says her first clear word: '*Bang!*'

In the Nativity Play Lawrence is going to be a shepherd, another Learning Experience for me because I wanted to be the star of everything and always assumed my children would too. But he doesn't mind. He has one line which Peter is helping him to practise.

'I'm the Angel Gabriel. I'm bringing Great News! What is it?'

'Biscuits!'

The play is fine, but the holidays wear us out. Getting dressed, sitting down for supper, starting supper, finishing supper, going upstairs at teeth-time, getting into pyjamas, getting into bed – *everything* is a battle. Peter and I keep snapping at each other, and it doesn't blow over. We're like two repelling magnets. I wish I'd never got married, or had children. In my notebook I write, *I feel like Oprah Winfrey in* The Color Purple. *My spirit is broken.*

At bedtime on the Monday, after three really bad days, I tell Lawrence: 'If you don't put on your pyjamas, I'm going to walk down the road and stay there. I just can't stand it.'

'Don't go, Mummy!'

I am now officially the Worst Mother in the World. But I still wish he'd just put on his fucking pyjamas.

On the Tuesday I bribe him with biscuits to leave for nursery on time, and afterwards, he shows me his entry in the Golden Book: *For coming into school every day with a smile.*

'That's lovely, darling! Well done!'

So the school gets the Jekyll and we get the Hyde. But I am a bit proud.

We go to play with with his friend Milo from Treetops, which Lawrence thinks is for his benefit, whereas it's for mine, because his mother Lucy is the only person round here I can tell when everything turns to shit. She's no more outwardly in control of things than I am, and has a new baby as well, but also enough energy to make flapjacks. Her kitchen smells of golden syrup. I take refuge there, and ask her: 'Why are children so fucking difficult?' And she says: 'God knows. Have another flapjack.'

And this is strangely comforting.

The boys play their favourite game, *Crash Bang*, and no one is wounded. I even manage to get my two out of there without meltdown. Then as soon as we get back, Lawrence starts screeching and hitting me. At bedtime I ask him to put on his pyjamas and he spits in my face. The books say *Don't reward bad behaviour with attention*, but what about when the children reward each other? He's winding Lydia up. And when *she* does something naughty, he gives her attention, loads of it. Well, you know what? Fuck this: I've had it. In a calm moment, or at least a brief gap between rows, I send him into the hall and shut the door. Almost immediately he calls out that he is sorry, comes back, finishes his dinner and sits on my lap for a bit of *I Spy Diggers*.

So I've solved the Great Parenting Problem! All I have to do is Never Engage in an Argument, Never Lose My Temper and Never Raise My Voice. And you know what really pisses me off? All the books say that: all of them.

'*The Great Truth you were seeking was right under your nose,*' says Peter, in his Zen Master voice.

'Shut up. Just shut up.'

Squirrels are vandalizing the bird-feeder. They come round in gangs and one keeps watch while the others force the lid off.

'Bugger off!' I shout at them. 'BUGGER OFF!!!'

'Bugger off!' shout Lydia and Lawrence. 'Bugger off!'

They repeat it a few more times, then Lawrence says: 'I think that's enough now.'

At breakfast he asks: 'Is it night-time in Australia?'

'Yes.'

'You're so clever, Mummy!'

The tantrums have mysteriously stopped. He comes home every day that week with a sticker for being Extra Good, and more or less at that exact moment, the same mysterious force turns Lydia into The Child From Hell. Outside the flower shop, while Lawrence is buying me a bunch of pink carnations – *Aaaah* – she stamps on a pot of hyacinths. I shout at her and, crying with rage, she does one of her faints. When she comes round, she resumes whining, and whines all the way home. (This makes Lawrence even sweeter.) After forty minutes of it I throw her in her cot, which I figure is better than hurling her out the window. Then I put the radio on and try to think about the Public Sector Borrowing Requirement, or Monica Lewinsky, or the weird mark on the carpet that looks like the prostate gland. *I cannot stand this any more.* I make a cup of tea and suddenly realize it's gone quiet. And there's no sign of Lawrence. I rush upstairs, holding my breath. When I peer round the door, he's under the bed retrieving Lydia's teddy slippers. She is standing in her cot, smiling. He says:

'I'm just going to fetch these to Lydia and I'll be right back.'

Over our debriefing that night I tell Peter: 'The boy's three, and his parenting technique is better than mine.'

'I'm not saying anything,' he says slowly. 'Not a thing.'

And he has inherited his father's gift for spin. When I shove him in his room for hitting me, he sweeps everything off the chest of drawers onto the floor.

'That's quite naughty, Mummy,' he admits. 'But it's quite good as well.'

'Oh, yes? Why's that?'

He gestures at the top of the chest. 'Because now this is all clean.'

I tell Katarina all our ups and downs. Without immediate relatives on hand she is someone to boast to, and when it goes pear-shaped she usually has a strategy. She has begun teaching them to count and is now teaching Lydia to say, '*May I?*' She gets the hang of it straight away.

'*May* I spill my milk?'

'*May* I jump off the table?'

'*May* I smack you, Mummy?' When she does do those things, I tell her off and Lawrence says: 'Good, Mummy!'

'Lydia!' I say. 'Stop hitting me!'

'Come here, Mummy,' says Lawrence. 'I'll deal with Lydia.'

'Aah, will you?'

'I'll kick her head off.'

Later he asks: 'Did you get angry with her?'

'Yes,' I say. 'Sometimes you get angry with children when they're naughty, but you love them just the same.'

'No!' he says vehemently. 'I *never* do!'

When I find a hairband in Lydia's pocket I ask, 'Can I borrow it?'

'No,' she says. 'But we can fight over it.'

There is an upside, however, to her stubbornness. *'The stubbornness that got us over the border and out of Lithuania,'* my father used to say, although he was born in Stamford Hill. That weekend we go to the woods, and she falls on a nettle. After a brief whimper, she wraps a dock leaf round her hand and carries on. The emigrating DNA combines impressively with Peter's robust, outdoors genes. His was the Dad that went Down the Gambia with a Thermos, mine the one for whom roughing it was a hard seat at the Edinburgh Fringe.

But can I cope? I'm glad I made notes during this period, because before, when someone told me their child had screamed for over an hour I didn't believe them. But here it is: *Lydia screamed for seventy mins this a.m. Finally Peter put her in her cot and she stopped.* She'd been to sleep, been fed. What the fuck was the matter??? I feel like the father of Woody Allen's character in *Radio Days: 'How do I know why there were Nazis? I don't know how a can opener works.'* I don't understand *anything*.

'It's all too difficult,' I tell Peter.

'You need to get out more.'

'You mean go away, because I'm such a bad mother.'

'No! You need a treat. You wanted to go to Paris with Claire. Go.'

'I can't leave the children. It wouldn't be right.'

'What's "right"? Denying yourself any pleasure in life?'

'I had a biscuit yesterday.'

'Right, that's it.'

I go and get out my passport, where I see a photo of a brazen, unfeeling woman. But Peter has arranged to leave work early on the Friday to collect the children, so I have to go. Besides, they are already drawing their impressions of the train.

The Eurostar is redolent of possibilities. I am a film director going to Rome to cast my new epic; I am a spy taking the night train to Belgrade to steal a microfilm; I am an heiress travelling to a secret assignation with the sexy lawyer who used to live in our road; I am – crying.

Claire gets on at Ashford. We have champagne and peanuts and I feel suddenly better. And I discover how much you can pack into a weekend without children in it. We buy lots of affordable, nice clothes, and have breakfast, coffee, lunch, tea, drinks and dinner – all without having to leave suddenly because of a squabble, or to rush home to change poohey clothes. Finally, Claire takes a picture of me having breakfast in bed: 'Just to prove you've done it.'

It is my Eiffel Tower.

16 I Am Not Alone

Summer is here, and we're heading for the Empty Quarter. We don't have the confidence or the energy to go abroad. Anyhow, we know that no package has been invented that takes care of a three and a two year old, while letting the adults read a book. I look at a Mark Warner brochure and reread the prices four times because I can't believe them.

'Why don't they tell you *this* in postnatal? Never mind breastfeeding.'

'What about that place Fiona went to? How much was that?'

'Forget it.'

Fiona is my new friend at school. She always takes her family on wonderful holidays, but then her husband works long hours so they save about £4,000 by not going out during the year.

'It was one of those resort things with a children's club.'

'Which we can't afford.'

'And . . .'

'What?'

'Sophie was just under the age limit, so they only managed to get rid of Tom.'

'Nightmare. Still, we've always got the park.'

'What, for six weeks? What shall we do? Oh, I forgot. You have a *job*. See you in September, then.'

September will be a Momentous Month. On the up side, Lydia is starting nursery. On the other hand, Katarina is going home to Slovakia. She may not be able to return. *Don't panic.*

'DON'T GO!!!!!!!!!!!!!!!!!!!!!!!'

'You'll be fine. Can you let go of my leg?'

In the beginning it was Maureen who stood between me and madness, now it's Katarina. Sometimes, at around seven, I come downstairs and find the children in bed and the table set with candles.

'Even if you're only having a takeaway,' she says, 'it will make you feel nice.'

She's turning herself into an excellent cook, graduating from slightly scary stews with Berlin Wall dumplings to aromatic stir-frys and home-made chicken nuggets, which Lawrence and Lydia make with her in an eggy assembly line. She's a keen viewer of Graham Norton and *Eurotrash*, and has 'got' English culture totally. The only thing she's missed is 'Noo-noo', her word for 'front bottom', being the vacuum cleaner in *Teletubbies*, but then I missed that as well. She has taught the kids '*hovno*' and '*hovienko*', Slovakian for 'pooh' and 'little tiny pooh'. And picking up that they're in danger of copying my less than clean language, she gets them to practise '*Domcek!*', a substitute expletive which is Slovakian for 'house'.

'It'll do you both good to have a break,' says Peter. He's right; we're too similar. Intelligent and imaginative, but proud and too easily hurt. When we start getting PMT at the same time, he retreats upstairs with his car magazines. Witnessing her disappointments with boyfriends is intolerably painful, like watching my younger self. That summer her father dies suddenly, just as mine did, and we have that in common too.

On the day of her departure, we take her to Victoria Coach Station. Lawrence cooperates, but Lydia won't hold my hand amidst the huddled masses, and when I tell her off, faints and does a wee on the concourse. At least it undercuts the emotion of the occasion. When I find Peter, he is standing, with husbandly foresight, next to the Pick 'n' Mix stall.

'Well done.'

'What?'

'Nothing.'

The front of the coach says *Praha*. It sounds somehow much further away than *Prague*. When she gets on, Peter and I are both tearful. Lawrence and Lydia finally tear themselves away from the Pick 'n' Mix and run after her calling, 'I love you!' and: 'You're my best friend in the whole world!'

The coach turns towards *Praha*, and we go home to practise being Proper Parents.

Thank God for nursery school, then. Lydia's been watching her brother for a year, so knows the routine. At the door she does not cry or hang onto my legs, but grabs an apron and heads straight for the dinosaur sandpit. At the end of the day, I arrive to find her releasing the other children to their mothers.

'Oh, no!' I say to the teacher.

'I don't mind!' she says.

'. . . And Luke, you can go,' says Lydia.

So: the good news is, she's more than ready for full-time nursery; the bad news is, she thinks she runs the place. But I don't care, because I now have five and a half hours of completely child-free time every day. I shall name this Golden Time, when only Very Important Things shall be done. I start by going to a cafe with a newspaper. It is so pleasurable that by the time I get to the second coffee I feel quite degenerate. If only I'd known it could take so little to have an *outrageously* good time, I'd have had kids earlier. At fourteen.

Coming out of the school gate at around this time I notice Jay, a mother I always smile at, though I don't know her, because she wears fantastic clothes and huge, sculptural earrings. She breezes through the other mummies leaving a vapour trail of pizazz, a catwalk in a sea of Boden. She is also a barrister who walks across Africa for mental health – other people's. She is talking to a small circle of mothers and nannies. Like a tourist passing Speakers' Corner, I slow down.

'Someone asked me the other day how I do it,' she's telling them. 'And I said, "It's simple: I put the children to bed in their school uniforms, and give them chocolate for breakfast in the car."' There is a ripple of laughter and approval. And a bell goes off in my head.

Other people take short cuts and 'cheat'. What if MOST of them do? What if it's – universal?

I go home and tell Peter: 'We're not the only ones.'

'The only ones what?'

'You know, who don't heat bottles, and drink while breastfeeding and – generally do it "wrong".'

'I'm sure we're not.'

'Yes, but what if everybody's like that? But none of us wants to own up? So we're all – sort of hiding. Thinking everyone else is doing it 'properly' – but no one is! Or almost no one.'

'What I can't stand is those bloody celebrities going on about how marvellous it all is, when they've got an army of cleaners and nannies.'

'Exactly! And the papers always telling us that if we put them in childcare they'll become shoplifters.'

'But if you stay at home with them you're "just a mother", so you can't win.'

'Yeah. I mean, have you ever met anyone who actually thinks they're doing a good job?'

'Mrs Thatcher always seems to sound quite pleased with how hers've turned out.'

'There you go. For the rest of us, it's taking short cuts, and having a drink instead of reading them a bedtime story, and feeling guilty all the time ... Like when we ate their Easter eggs—'

'You didn't feel guilty.'

'Yes, I did. Anyhow, it was your idea. Look, shut up. It's like abortion used to be. It just took one or two women to "confess". What if I could somehow say that? That it's OK. We could all "come out".'

'You're saying it now.'

'No. I mean to lots of people. To everyone who's sick

217

of being pressurized to feel *nurturing* and *fulfilled* twenty-four hours a day. I'm going to start a magazine.'

I then outline my vision for the most stunning and brilliant publication ever, which I shall edit from a beautiful office with white Bakelite phones, and a curved, art deco desk. And a view. It'll be on sale in all the newsagents, and all the schools, and all the playgroups, and reach every mother in the land.

'Great idea,' says Peter.

'There's just one problem. I need five million pounds.'

'Ah. What are you going to call it, anyway?'

It's something Annie used to say. We stayed with her in Australia. She started her own business when her children were small, and when their father died, she managed brilliantly. But she never thought that. She was always worrying about fucking up, agonizing dreadfully in a way we – then childless – found baffling and hilarious. At the first sign of trouble – one of the kids refusing to do their homework or whatever – she'd turn to us and say: 'Am I a Bad Mother?' And we'd say: 'How would *we* know?'

'So . . . here's the thing. What if other women are also *thinking* they're Bad Mothers, while actually being – like Annie – perfectly good?'

'God knows women waste megawatts of energy beating themselves up.'

'Exactly!'

'Well, you could always do it on the net.'

'Oh no. I hate all that. And I'm completely untechnical, you know that.'

A week later I'm sitting in the office of RedSpy, who build skiing and motoring websites. None of them is a woman or has kids.

'Great! It sounds great,' says Jay, the boss.

'What, you – think you can do it?'

'A website? Sure. What d'you want on it?

I show them my sheet of A4, with 'Extreme Breastfeeding' written at the top.

'This is a section which people can contribute to, about the strangest or worst places they've ever done it.'

'Cool,' says Sam, the designer.

'And I want to add something about sending a team to the next Olympics.' The young man who was answering the phone has stopped answering the phone and is now joining in.

'And, um, I thought we could have a bit called "Tantrum of the Week" – where mothers describe how they've lost it, sort of thing.'

'Great. And—?'

'That's as far as I've got. I thought I could write some features, and maybe commission some.'

'OK, and you'll probably need a forum.'

'What's that?'

'We'll show you. And how are you going to fund it?'

'I have no idea.'

'OK. Great.'

I'm paying them the money we've put on one side in case we ever go on holiday again, so I spend carefully. I write a piece called *How To Be Less Mumsy*, and one called *How To Do Less*, and a survey that asks, *How often do you get time to yourself?* And *When it all goes wrong, where do you turn?* My friend Vida, who brought up her two sons in Italy where they ran wild, has written a book in which her neighbour describes her as '*Una Madre Terribile*', and she gives me an extract from it.

I have no pictures. My only idea for the home page is an icon of the Virgin Mary rolling her eyes. After looking at 200 Virgin Marys at a picture library, I get an image in my head of a woman with a cocktail glass, only instead of an olive or a glacé cherry on the rim, there's a dummy. Sam, the designer, and Becky, the photographer, go off and shoot it. They've never seen a dummy before, so I carefully describe what one looks like in case they buy a shop mannequin by mistake. The model is Sam's flat-mate, Toni. Despite having no experience of mother-hood, she manages to strike just the right attitude of resignation and fatigue. The forum I call *Retell Therapy*, because sharing a problem makes you feel better. Then I send a press release headed *'Join the Bad Mothers Club!'* to a few newspapers and chain myself back to my double buggy.

17 Just Press 'Start'

Sunday morning. Lawrence wakes us to order milk from the twenty-four-hour room service he thinks we have.

'Can you get it yourself?'

'No!'

'Yes, you can. There's a bottle in the door of the fridge. Go and look.'

'I want it warm!'

This is Katarina's fault. We never warmed bottles till she came along.

'Tired. Please let me sleep,' begs Peter.

'What time is it?'

'5.30.'

'Fuck . . .'

'Please don't make me get up. If I have to get up now I'll die.' He often gets up first. If I admitted how often, the tiny wisp of my credibility would dissolve altogether. On the other hand, he is more of a Morning Person.

'Mummmmeeeeeee!'

Lawrence is also a Morning Person. He is at the bedside now, pulling at me.

'OK. Wait . . .'

I accompany him down to the kitchen, get the bottle and put it in the microwave. He presses the button.

'I want to do it!'

'OK, hang on . . . Now, see that one? OK, press that one – not that one – then "Start".'

Ping!

'I did it!'

'Now, just give it a little shake . . .'

'I did it!' He is delighted with himself. I put on *Fireman Sam* and get a lie-in until seven. What did they used to have on the charity posters? *Give a man a fish and feed him for a day. Teach him to fish and feed him for life.*

'Peter! If we teach them to do more things for themselves, we get more time off.'

'Mmm. Very good.'

'There's a clear relationship between this ridiculous mollycoddling, driving them everywhere and whatnot, and the fact that parents are so worn out. We're actually disabling our own children!'

I remember a story told me by a bloke I worked with, about his son 'having to have' a mobile phone. The son, aged fourteen, had gone to stay at a mate's. 'When I asked what they did and all that,' he said, 'he said they'd rung up this girl they knew – at 2 a.m.! And she invited them round! I said, "Er, and did you go?" And he said, "Nah. We didn't know how to get there."'

'You see? No initiative! Now, if the Bad Mothers Club could somehow encourage parents to – *Peter*?'

'Zzzzzzzzzzzzz.'

But he does agree really. And the next stage of our children's self-reliance develops the same way.

Their nursery lies on the right fork of two busy roads, and to avoid crossing where there is no crossing, we walk up the left fork, then cut across a bit of green the children call Railway Park, because it has an edged path down the middle a bit like a mini train track. Usually Lawrence runs along it being a train while I push Lydia. At the end, however, is a 'kissing gate', the sort of 'amenity' favoured by the Dulwich Estate to remind us all of when it was called *Dill Wysse* and had cows and sheep roaming through it instead of under-slept women with pushchairs. With a double buggy, forget it. You have to go the long way round, or move to Wales. Even with a single, it's infuriating. I have to tip Lydia out, keeping the buggy on the fronts of its wheels like a trick skater, and can negotiate the barrier if I position the buggy in *exactly* the right place, at *exactly* the right angle and swing the gate *just so*. I feel like one of those people who helps horses to mate.

'Mummy don't swear. You're very naughty,' says Lawrence.

'Sorry. It's just so fucking annoying, that's all!'

The children are aghast. But I have the solution.

'All right, that's it.'

'We're sorry, Mummy.'

Poor things: they're so used to being shouted at.

'No, no, I'm not blaming you! We're just going to walk from now on, that's all.'

'No *BUGGY* . . .?!'

The next day we set off, wheel-less, as nature intended. Allowing a few extra minutes, we get there easily. I have to be an express train or a goods wagon for part of the journey, but it's a small price to pay. Less than two years ago I pushed them up the hill from Maureen's, breathing like an obscene phone caller all the way. Now they're running. Lydia is quite fast. At a birthday party on Wandsworth Common she suddenly strikes out across the grass, like James Garner in *The Great Escape*, and has to be retrieved by one of the dads. On the way home from nursery it gets worse. One afternoon she outstrips me and by the time I catch up, limping, she is in conversation with an elderly woman who has got out of her car 'because the child was on her own'.

'She's not on her own,' I say. I have sent Lawrence on

ahead to explain this, but he has become absorbed in a ladybird which he spotted on a leaf twenty feet away with his four-year-old eyesight.

'There was no one here.'

'*I'm* here.'

'Yes, but she was on her own—'

'SHE IS NOT "ON HER OWN". I AM HERE. I AM HER MOTHER. I CANNOT KEEP UP WITH HER BECAUSE I HAVE A BAD KNEE.'

This is true. I have tripped over some of that nylon binding that the florist likes to leave on the pavement like a rabbit trap, and can no longer run. The woman gets back into her car, to be superior all the way back to My Generation Knows Better Land.

Fine. I've got nothing to worry about except Sports Day, when the school punishes you for your misdemeanours throughout the year by making you run the Mothers' Race. This is our second year. Last year, the Goddess of Bad Mothers smiled on me and – about thirty seconds before the start – sent forth a plague of rain. But I don't expect to be lucky twice. Also, I have two children there now, so will need all my cartilage to limp back and forth between events.

I've always been a crap runner, but it never mattered. My parents understood why I spent games periods hiding in the lavatories; they'd done much the same thing. For my mother, being Bad at Games is even a creative *sine qua non*. But now we've got someone in the family who LIKES sport, someone I don't want to disappoint. Which is worse, to bow out pathetically without even trying? Or make the effort, cripple my knee, and run the risk of being given an '*I Tried my Best*' sticker by the Head? Eventually I decide a stay in an orthopaedic ward will be a small price to pay for just one proud glance from my daughter. The teacher shouts, '*Go!*'

I leg it like fury, scattering babies and cool bags, and, to my astonishment, come third. Lydia wins her race easily, despite missing the start by gazing in the opposite direction and being the only girl.

Lawrence's races are taking place simultaneously on the other side of the field so I limp across to where his class is doing their 'stick and ball' race, a sort of hockey dribble, just in time to see him lose the ball, throw down his stick and hurl himself in a rage onto the grass. Peter, who is still adjusting the wideshot facility on the digicam, goes after him. I feel humiliated; this reflects on ME. I can see Peter trying to persuade him to come back for the next race, and Lawrence getting more and more furious with himself. I catch his teacher's eye, and look ashamed.

'Don't worry,' she says. 'I've lost three that way already.'

Lydia skips up, festooned with Winner stickers and sucking a triumphant ice lolly.

'Did you win, Lawrence?'

'NO, I DIDN'T!!!'

Never mind designer babies. Can we just have two at the same level? I can't praise Lydia without making Lawrence feel worse. But I don't want her to grow up thinking everything brilliant she does is just ordinary, and that to get any fuss made of her she has to be Jonathan Miller.

I tell Peter: 'This is your fault for making us have them too close together.'

'Divide and Rule,' he says.

So we walk home in two teams of two, one of us to distract Lawrence from the ball and stick element of Life, and the other to tell Lydia she is a star.

Half-term. Fiona invites me and the kids to the Royal Horticultural Society Garden at Wisley.

'I'm a member!' she says, in case I think she never does anything outside school.

We set off down the A3. Halfway down, squabbling breaks out and Lydia undoes her seat belt to get a better shot at her brother. I can see her in the rear-view mirror, but cannot stop. Anyhow, I'm in the fast lane.

'Do your seat belt up NOW! *NOW!* 'She throws a book at me: a board book. 'OW!!' I am so angry that when we get there I haul her out and smack her. Fiona and her two watch silently. These were the people I was hoping might one day invite us on holiday. Holiday to Guantanamo.

'Who'd like an apple?' says Fiona sweetly. Lawrence and Lydia take one, the first time they've ever accepted fruit without complaint.

We go round the garden, and everyone is pretty good. Fiona has brought a picnic, and afterwards we decide that the children definitely deserve an ice cream. There are tables in the cafe area, but they're all full, so we sit on the steps facing the lawn, with our backs to the dining gentlefolk.

'Keep the noise down, though,' I say. 'People are having their lunch.' There is a slightly tense atmosphere, as if the children are somehow out of bounds. And one couple is already glaring at us.

'Ssh, be very good now,' I say. But this is a mistake, because Lydia – with a wild look on her face – throws her welly over her shoulder, and it lands right in the glaring lady's lunch. Thank God she's too old to come over and thump me, is what I think first, swiftly followed by, this child has embarrassed me in public for the last time. She gets another smack and I promise Fiona never to accept an invitation from her again. I feel dreadful, as if I have poison in my veins. I hate myself beyond imagining. No one in the history of the universe has ever been a worse mother than I am now. What can I do, promise never to do it again? Or am I like an alcoholic, too weak to have any self-control? I am like an alcoholic in one respect: the next day, and for weeks afterwards, I feel the need to confess.

'Have I told you I smacked my child? Twice?' I want to tell people in the newsagent's, at the park, over drinks. What am I looking for? Some kind of punishment, then I can feel absolved. And once again, I get my wish.

The Bad Mothers Club press release has been picked up by the *Daily Mail*, who interview me, Kath, and three other friends with stories to tell. On the day it comes out, I get a call from ITV's *This Morning*. Three of us go into the studio, and I tell the story of Our Day Out At Wisley. Of course, before I can get to the part about no one being perfect and the whole point of Bad Mothers Club, the presenter says: 'If you can't look after children, you shouldn't have had them.'

When I get home, the website has received 200 messages from mothers saying they know how I feel. And they keep coming.

'I think,' says Peter, 'you may have struck a bit of a chord.'

18 The Cheeseless Tunnel:
Why Parents are Stupider than Rats

Lawrence, two at the time, wants 20p to ride on the
Postman Pat van outside Sainsbury's. It's the usual
worthless effort: a minimal rocking to and fro – hardly
enough to loosen your nappy – while the speakers blast
out that bloody awful song. A Formula One, Supercrash,
or riddle-you-with-bullets arcade game I could see the
point of, but this? No way worth 20p. And I know that
after one ride – because they're so damn short – he'll
want another. And two rounds of that tune will put me
in a very bad mood. So clearly, to say No is best for all
concerned. I know how to say No. You just put your lips
together and—

'Postman Pat! Postman Pat!'

'No way. Come on, we've shopping to get.'

'Postman Pat! Postman Pat! Aargh!'

'No! Come *on!*'

'I want Postman Pat! *Aaaarrgghh!*'

Sympathetic looks from fellow parents are replaced,

as I drag him away from the cause of his anguish, by more perturbed stares. I try the advice from the books: '*Do not reward bad behaviour by paying attention to it. Ignore the outburst and carry on with the task in hand.*' So I get Lydia in the trolley and move purposefully towards the automatic doors, which open and close again, leaving the screaming Lawrence on the edge of the car park. A woman in a hairband gives me a glare.

'*Muu-mmeee!*' he screams, without moving. A mother who refuses him 20p for a Postman Pat ride is clearly not worth following anywhere.

I grab him off the forecourt, stuffing him too roughly into the second trolley seat so that he cries even more, and grimly begin the ordeal of manoeuvring a flailing, scarlet toddler – and now a weeping one year old as well – down the aisle. I do this, obviously, for the satisfaction of those perfect, childless shoppers who believe that parents take their children to supermarkets, not to do any shopping but to fight. My frustration is exacerbated by self-loathing because I've bashed his hand on the edge of the trolley. As we stop at Pasta, I'm thinking of telling Peter – *again* – that the whole thing has been a mistake; I shouldn't have become a mother after all, and both children should be removed from me and brought up by nuns. By the time we get to the Bakery section, my guilt is such that I have to buy them a doughnut each, and then I need one – well, two – because I've used up all my blood sugar having my tantrum. We all nibble away with relief, covering ourselves and the rest of the food in sugar. At the checkout we are all calm, and Lydia is dazzling shoppers with her film star beam. But when we come out: 'Postman Pat! Postman Pat! *Aaaarrrrgggghhh!*'

And they ask why we give them sweets.

Talking to my friend Harriet, whose son Jack is a bit older, I discover there's a wonderful technique known to more experienced parents which isn't in any of the books. It's called Lying. You just load the *Lies for Windows* software and off you go!

'Oh, dear, it's broken. Never mind!'

Or:

'I've got no change! I'm really sorry, kids . . .'

It's amazing how empowering dishonesty can be. Harriet says she has another friend who deals thus with the ice-cream van: 'As soon as she hears that music, she says: *"Oh, sorry kids: they're playing that tune that means they've run out of ice cream."*' At this I fall silent, recognizing when I'm in the presence of talent.

But, as usual, this new gun in my armoury is ineffective in the next battle. Peter comes in from work, where he is reviewing cars.

'Hello,' I say. 'What did you do today?'

'Compared the Aston Martin Vanquish with the Lamborghini Murelago. How about you?'

'I took Lawrence to play at Daniel's, and he wouldn't put on his shoes.'

'What did you do?'

'Shouted *"GET YOUR SHOES ON!!!"* about 500 times.'

'Did it work?'

'No.'

'Ah. A Cheeseless Tunnel.'

'And Daniel's mother's a child psychologist, so . . .'

'Eek!'

'Exactly. In the end I dragged him to the car in his socks. He cried all the way home, and I felt awful.' I pour us a drink. 'What's a Cheeseless Tunnel?'

'Well . . . you know those experiments where rats learn to crawl through a maze, or push open a catch, to retrieve a piece of cheese at the end of a tunnel? If the cheese is taken away, they eventually give up. But people don't. They keep trying, even after what they're doing has been proven not to work. That's the Cheeseless Tunnel.'

'So what you're saying is that parents are stupider than rats.'

'Basically.'

'So how do I get Lawrence to put on his shoes?'

'I have no idea.'

'Well, what use are you, then? Go away.'

'On the other hand, though, if people were like rats, we would never have had the Panama Canal.'

'Or the jet engine.'

'Or the disposable nappy, which can hold forty-eight litres of baby urine before it explodes in a blizzard of wet crystals.' (Do not try this in an enclosed space such as a lift.)

'So man can do all these amazing things . . .'

'. . . But can't get a three year old to put on his shoes.'

Peter considers the matter for a few moments. 'What about encouragement and reward?'

'You mean another weekend in Paris?'

'Not you: him.'

'Oh.'

'Try noticing when he does something you want him to do and give him a reward.'

'Try noticing when I've had a shit day and bring me some chocolate.'

'No, it's Positive Reinforcement, you see, it—'

'Just leave me alone!'

This, therefore, is why two adults – one or both of

whom may have been educated to degree level – believe that if they shout, '*Eat your broccoli!*' enough times, the child will eat it. Rats know better.

The whole vegetable nightmare, and the insane levels of bribery it drives you to, is brilliantly satirized in Kes Gray and Nic Sharratt's great surrealist work, *Eat Your Peas*. Starting quite rationally with offers of extra pudding, Daisy's mother quickly progresses to increasingly outlandish promises of animals, bikes, chocolate factories and entire theme parks, in the hope of getting the wretched girl to eat her peas. And even that doesn't work.

I tell Lawrence: 'When you've eaten your broccoli you can have a video.' And he counters: 'I don't *want* a video.' But it worked last time! Bugger, bugger, *bugger* it! And *that's* followed by: 'I'm tired.'

In other words, what he'd really like is to go to bed early without any telly. Well I don't know about you, but in my day that was a punishment.

The Golden Rule being Not to Disagree in Front of Them, tension and confusion are racked up further by our failure to agree on the correct technique. In fact, our worst rows now invariably start this way.

'If you eat your broccoli . . .' begins Peter.

'When. It's *when*.'

'Whatever.'

'No, not "whatever". You're supposed to remove the element of choice. That's the point!'

'Look, can we just get through the meal?'

Lawrence and Lydia see the parental fissure opening up, and ruthlessly boot it wide open.

'She kicked me!'

'He was going to steal my drink!'

'Well done,' says Peter. 'Happy now?'

We are worn out. There is surely no other job in which you effectively take an exam every day. Every *hour*. And all your rough workings are shown. Not only are results consistently inconsistent – what works one day will suddenly for no reason not work the next – but even the *attempt* to follow some kind of strategy is cruelly exposed. Running for the bus and missing it is tolerable; being seen panting to a halt by the passengers is not. When that happens I have to run past the stop to pretend I was running for some other reason, like my health. The children hearing us debate our methods is embarrassing, like being seen in the car picking your nose.

Peter – and I have observed that this seems to be a *male* thing – will sometimes *alter*, shall we say, certain previously agreed parameters, in the interests of an Easy Life. But as we all know, this is Short Termism, which

Makes Things Worse in the End. When I was five, my parents had a huge row after my dad let us have ice lollies, which we weren't allowed. We went on and on at him, and because Mum had gone out, he gave in. But we were still eating them when she came back. '*I thought we agreed*,' she kept wailing, '*I thought we agreed!*' Shortly afterwards they were divorced.

My own relationship is similarly corroded by the acid of childish determination. Trying to go to my sister's, I ring – another thing we disagree about – to say we're running a bit late.

'Where are you?' she says.

'We're still trying to get them into the car.' Her astonishment, for she is not yet a mother, can be heard in the awed silence echoing down the line.

I remember this from when they first began to resist being put in the pushchair. The body goes stiff and flat like an ironing board, with red, square-mouthed face at one end, and sharp, kicking legs at the other. You practically have to punch them in the stomach to fold them in. And now, with time ticking away, we're in Car Seat Hell, battling steroidally strong, whirling limbs with the added option of back strain. To twist round, lean down and get them into the car seat, the doing up of which – as with an epidural, requires the subject to be *still* – demands a combination of determination and forbearance that would defeat Jesus. And he didn't have a bad back.

'Just get in the seat, will you?' begs Husband, in Defeated Tone of Voice.

'NO-O-O-O-O-O!'

Me: 'Bloody get in your seat!'

'NO-O-O-O-O-O!'

Him: 'Get in the car, and – we'll get an ice cream on the way.'

'What? To eat in the car? You are joking!'

'Well, you do it then.' (Husband returns to house.)

Weekends are a flashpoint anyhow, even without involving the car. Peter, who spent his childhood trudging up and down fells, likes to spend Saturday and Sunday lying about reading the papers and watching films. I, who spent my childhood at the cinema, lurch through the house clutching at my throat and gasping because I hate being cooped up. The park is only a short walk away. He says: 'The children are happy just pottering around at home.' Which indeed they are – until, with their energy building up like a pressure cooker, they blow their tops and start a war.

As they throw punches I say: 'See?' And he says, in his little-known, Basil Fawlty voice: 'Right! Mummy wants to go to the park.' So everyone's clear about who's inflicting this torture. Although we can get out of the house with less equipment than when they were babies, the negotiation involved is more exhausting. We reattach hoods, get out hats, wellies, gloves, water, a carrier bag for worms and a snack, *then* begin the rounds of talks. Lydia, to be fair, can be convinced in less than an hour – so long as she can bring a bag full of soft toys which she will get tired of carrying as soon as we've left the house. Lawrence, however, treats the invitation as husbands do the information that they're to pop in for a drink with the neighbours: as an assault on his precious spare time. The fact that he loves the park once he gets there, is no help. He glances a millimetre away from *Tom and Jerry* and informs me: 'It's my day off.'

Peter says: 'If you come to the park you can have a croissant.'

'Well, what's the point of the exercise then?' I say. 'Why bother ever doing anything healthy?'

'Can we just get out of the house?'

'At least consult me before you make these stupid offers . . .'

'OK, you do it then . . .' (Husband returns to sofa.)

He is also conducting an ongoing bribe, involving squash. Influenced by my mother's squash phobia, I don't want them to have their water – and therefore their teeth – ruined by it. He claims to be worried about their 'fluid intake'. It's got to the point now where we each spy on whoever's doing the drinks.

'Oi, no!' I bark, seeing the pink bottle out of the corner of my eye. Then while I'm opening the wine, he sneaks Lydia her fix. Lawrence will at least settle for fizzy water, though even there Peter has to get back at me by observing: 'I read somewhere that the carbon dioxide is bad for their teeth.'

He's never read an article about nutrition in his life. He thinks he's clever, going behind my back with the squash, but I do most of the shopping and on the next run I'm going to forget to buy any. Ha-*hah*!

Lawrence knows his father will negotiate endlessly for an Easy Life.

'I'll sit down at the table if I can have a biscuit,' he tells him, as I am about to serve supper. We're getting to the point where in order to achieve anything, we'll have to get in teams of mediators.

And that still leaves us the problem of reverse bargaining. When I say to Lawrence: 'You can have a sweet if you do your teeth afterwards' – he only has to keep his end of the bargain *after* he's had the treat. So not surprisingly, I get screwed. When I say: 'You won't get a sweet next time,' he replies: 'I don't care.' Of course, when it comes to next time he does care, and I get stuffed again. Peter says it's because kids, unlike adults, don't appreciate anything once it's in the past. They never say: 'Remember that time I was bawling my eyes out and you bought me a toy car? Cheers for that!'

Similarly, Lydia goes to a friend's house to play, but fails to keep her end of the deal, which is to put her own clothes back on to go home. If I explain beforehand: 'When I come to get you, promise you'll get ready without a fuss?' she nods dutifully and says: 'Yes, Mummy. I promise.'

Cut to: Me arriving at friend's house to find her dressed as a fairy or a princess or a lion, or with nothing on at all. And it always follows the same pattern: 'Lydia, time to go. Can you get dressed, please?'

Lydia (running upstairs): 'Ha-ha-ha-ha!'

One afternoon, I promise Lawrence we will get Lydia and definitely be back in time for *The Simpsons*, which I want to watch myself. But not wanting the Other Mother to think our lives are ruled by television, I say: 'We can't be late. We've got someone coming round at six.'

'Who, Mummy? Who?'

'Er . . . Katarina.'

Lydia drops everything. 'Katarina! Katarina!'

And while the Other Mother is kindly searching for Lydia's socks, I whisper: 'Not really. But if you come now you can watch *The Simpsons*.'

'THE SIMPSONS!!!!' yells Lydia, making a fool of me in front of the Other Mother, and becoming so excited she forgets about getting dressed altogether.

Which is, I believe, where we came in.

I have no answers to any of this, so I'll just close on this thought: the three most devoted couples I know don't have kids. On the other hand, when they argue, who is there to blame?

19 A Little Light Bedtime Reading

Peter's sister and her boyfriend have offered to have both children to stay the night. The excitement on all our parts is too much. Jessica is their favourite person. She has a dog, a cat and endless patience. What's more, her two sons are nearly thirty and still speaking to her.

Unable to make a decision about a hotel, we decide to have dinner and see a film.

'There's the new Jack Nicholson.'

'Sure! Anything with him in it.'

On the way, we read the blurb in the paper.

'*A retiring police chief pledges to catch the killer of a young child.*'

'Ah.'

But: '*Jack Nicholson in a tormenting, riveting performance.*'

We love Jack Nicholson. It's harrowing, but the harrowingness is offset by Vanessa Redgrave doing a Swedish accent. And anyhow, we have worse visions in our heads.

A Little Light Bedtime Reading

I remember once trying to defend *The Silence of the Lambs* to a man who didn't like horror films.

'Um, well, I think when you see a film with a monster in it, and you experience your fear, and the monster is killed or conquered or whatever, at the end, it's quite, you know, satisfying,' I said. And he replied: 'I think that's entirely fatuous.'

But he was wrong. That book single-handedly rescued a holiday in a dark, gloomy house in France when it rained all the time and the 'swimming pool' was five feet across and inflatable. We had only one copy, so took turns. I read the last chapter locked in the car, with the rest of the family circling outside like wolves. But that's not the reason I respect Thomas Harris and his kind. He knows the insides of people's heads are not fundamentally nice and sweet. And of course it's not true only of grown-ups.

Children love stories about monsters; everyone knows that. They are avid for horrible, beastly tales and fascinated by violence. But obviously, there's violence and violence. Lawrence and Lydia are still at the age where they think it would be hilarious to be hit by a lorry and be 'squashed as flat as a pancake. Or an ice-cream van!' – the prospect of being hit at thirty mph by a ton of strawberry cornets being utterly thrilling.

But it's hard to gauge the bedtime reading matter

just right. Well, it would probably be easier if we stuck to the books labelled for their age. But we get bored. Also, children don't progress in their taste in an incremental, linear way – any more than adults do. They're extremely nostalgic for some of the first stories we ever read to them – and no wonder; several are absolutely brilliant. But then there are the books which they *can* read themselves, or will soon be able to, but which they still insist we read to them. And these are often the ones we like the least.

Chief offenders at this stage are the *Mr Men* books, with their so-called 'plots' in which the main character always goes for a walk and meets the other characters. The aim seems to be to stamp out individuality. Everyone ignores *Mr Noisy* until he learns to be quiet. *Mr Messy* gets 're-educated' into being tidy by communist, Cultural Revolution-style thugs.

'*Neat and Tidy*,' they say, '*Tidy and Neat.*'

Doesn't it just make your blood run cold?

Or Lydia wants *The Lion King*, which I'll use any excuse to get out of. Peter, being nicer, tends to give in, but speeds up more ruthlessly than I do. He can do *Lion King II* in 108 seconds. I don't know which is worse, that, or Disney's cutesy 'retellings' of the classics. I can't wait to see how they'll do *Madame Bovary*: '*In ancient France, a humble country doctor's wife longed to seek beyond the simple pleasures of village life . . .'* Or have they got onto Shake-speare yet? *'In ancient Denmark, a noble young prince sought to avenge his father's death while asking himself some pretty tough questions along the way . . .'*

This is why we've sent the children to schools where they'll be hot-housed, so they can hurry up and learn to read to themselves. And it's starting to work already, up to a point. Lawrence will read Lydia a few pages – of something pretty infantile – just to show that he can do something she can't. But it only lasts for a few minutes. So, until they're completely self-sufficient, one way to keep control over bedtime reading is to make up our own stories, as both my parents – effortlessly, it seemed – used to do. As well as spinning fictions out of thin air, my mother told tales from Greek myths, opera and folklore, although looking back on it she did rather tend towards the macabre. She was very keen on Tosca, and I can remember the sinking feeling after the firing squad scene, when the lover didn't get up. She was also quite fond of Cupid and Psyche, in which Psyche is tricked into losing Cupid for ever by his jealous mother Venus, and then there were her versions of reports by Mayhew, the pioneering Victorian journalist also not known for his happy endings. I've never forgotten the interview with the infant watercress seller, who could not play in the park because she had to work from dawn till dusk for a few farthings, or starve. The fact that the park outside in which she stood was our own playground, made it all the more heart-rending.

My father, being less intellectual, created cheerier narratives such as the story of Mr Today and his friends – Mr Today's body was a calendar which he flipped over every morning – who went on a journey through the Forest of Feelings to the Palace of Pleasure, which was guarded by fierce birds named after an – at the time – well-known brand of shampoo. The saga continued over many nights, taking whichever direction he fancied at the time. At our urgings he wrote some of it down, but we couldn't understand why it was never finished.

Because it's bloody exhausting, that's why, improvising a story on the spot, then trying to recall the exact details on subsequent nights. On holiday at the seaside I have a go, but the best I can manage is a kind of imperious, superannuated mermaid, a bit like Margaret Thatcher with a tail. The Sea-Fairy Queen has sea horses for servants and I invent her as a way to stop the children running along the sea wall and falling onto the rocks on the other side. I tell them she'll push them off the wall if they disobey, because she owns the beach.

Bizarrely, they like the idea of this scaly despot, and I am forced to think up more adventures for her, such as setting impossible tasks for her daughter's suitors and so on. But the effort wears me out. Peter does a little better, with improvised meanderings that involve Lawrence and Lydia and whatever objects – a flying boat, a diamond potty, a chocolate tree – that they want him to include. But this too cannot be kept up for long. So, guiltily, we resort to tapes. But these do not produce the hoped-for results; Lydia likes *Puffin Poems*, while Lawrence will only be quiet for *The Greek Myths*. Fights break out over whose turn it is to choose, so that when we come up for final kisses, *Theseus and the Minotaur* pales by comparison. I yell: 'GO TO SLEEEEP!!!'

And, eventually, they do.

'Why read the Twelve Labours of bloody Hercules when you can live it,' says Peter, reeling out of their room.

Around this time, I see a copy of *My Family and Other Animals* in a charity shop which – due to my previous indifference to the charms of the furry and feathered fraternity – I've never read. It suits us perfectly. Most of the characters are totally self-absorbed, especially the sneering Larry, who complains constantly and sets the house on fire, and Leslie, who wants to shoot dear little Gerry's pets. Gerry reminds me of Lawrence; he's lately begun stopping to examine spiders and shield bugs on the way to school, and we have a stag beetle in our salt dish, though it hasn't moved for a while.

'Do stag beetles like salt, Mummy?'

'Yes, but not that much.'

The whole Durrell household has so captivated me that I desperately want to be Mrs D, who drifts through the chaos without ever losing her temper, and have started to fantasize about moving to Corfu in the 1950s. Eventually, though, even this literary treat starts to pall. They lose interest in Gerry's last tutor, a hunchbacked, pathological liar and like Sheherezade, we have to come up with a new plot, or die.

Thank God we've still got so many of our own childhood favourites. Catherine Storr's *Clever Polly and the Stupid Wolf* I have kept for over thirty years. Polly and the Wolf have a relationship characterized by humour and ambivalence. The Wolf tries to be brilliant and predatory, but is stupid and lazy. He comes round on various pretexts to try and eat her, but she always outwits him. She feels slightly sorry for him, though, a bit like Lisa Simpson with Homer. Indeed, the sitcommy quality of their escapades goes down well, and, emboldened by my success with Polly, I decide to try and train them to like everything else by the same writer.

Here's my old copy of *Lucy,* a girl who wants to be a boy, and to prove herself catches a gang of burglars. The only problem comes when she stows away in their van and ends up having to escape from their hideout.

'But of course *you* wouldn't do this, would you?' I point out.

'We would if the burglars were bad.'

'Well, no, you see, because it might be dangerous. It *would* be dangerous.'

'But Lucy can do it.'

It was written, of course, in 1962.

In *Lucy Runs Away*, she gets so sick of not being a boy that she gets a train all the way to Cornwall – again by herself – and outwits the guard who thinks she's escaping her cruel parents and offers to call the welfare. On the beach she saves an old man from drowning by calling the lifeguard, but I rather overshadow this triumph by emphasizing the risks inherent in getting trains to distant places without adults. At least nowadays they're so often delayed the parents would easily catch up. But I feel denigrating Lucy's autonomy is a pity, because I do want them to be independent – not least so I can have some of my life to myself while I'm young enough to enjoy it. Anyhow, it's with my next choice that I get out of my depth.

Polly, the Giant's Bride is about a young girl on holiday with her family in Birling Gap who meets a giant. He starts off politely enough, by giving her a stone bracelet and ring. But the ring and bracelet won't come off, and then he starts sending her horrible, creepy notes. In other words, he's an enormous stalker. 'Eights and Over' says the blurb on the back, not, as in Lydia's case, 'Five And Under' – i.e. four. I have a sinking feeling as I read it, for *Polly, the Giant's Bride* is, I remember now, absolutely terrifying.

Lydia's sitting bolt upright in her bed. Her face is becoming more and more anxious; she's nearly crying. No, she's not, she's – gripped, and wants to hear it again. And – again. Thank God it does actually have a happy ending, and the heroine is not assaulted by a man who jumps out from behind the cliffs with an unfeasibly large cock.

Shaken by my lack of judgement, I over-correct, and try to repair the damage with *Robin*, which though by the same author is the polar opposite of *Polly*, written in a completely different style, with long passages of description and very little action except towards the end, when Robin rescues a storm-tossed ship by dialling the coast-guard, all thanks to his magic shell. You see what I mean? He is ever so slightly soppy. And inevitably by chapter three I am skipping more and more, and flipping the pages furtively to see if there might be a helicopter chase or machine-gun attack I'd forgotten. But no, Robin continues to go for walks and examine his magic shell, to not entirely surprising taunts from his older brother and sister. So I resort to trying to make the thing more exciting by varying the modulation of my voice. However this doesn't help much, as I find that yelling the line, *"ARE YOU MAGIC?!!" he asked the shell!'* only irritates my audience more.

Then I find our copy of Roald Dahl's *Boy*. The dead mouse in the sweetie jar is possibly the most famous bit, but they like even better the section in which Roald's nose is torn off while being driven by his sister, in the days when you bought a car and then taught yourself to drive. Being squeamish, I have to delegate this bit to Peter, or read while looking away. The same goes for the removal of Roald's adenoids – with no anaesthetic – and the chapter where poor Ellis is stabbed by the doctor lancing his boil. In fact, the whole book is full of people being hurt in various appalling ways. It is ideal for children.

Peter and I discuss this factor over a bottle one night, and feel that they're bound to enjoy the sequel, *Going Solo*, which takes the writer from England to East Africa. But what we've forgotten, having last read it pre-parenthood, is that halfway through, there's a murder. We're all right with the servant's wife being grabbed by a lion, because she jumps out of its mouth, dusts down her dress and walks away. But as I read on, I get a bit of a feeling that something fairly unpleasant is about to happen with a sword. It's funny; you'd think you'd remember someone being decapitated. Hearing that war has been declared, Dahl's brave and loyal servant Mdisho is desperate to help. When Dahl returns to the house and finds his sword missing, he rightly suspects the worst. Mdisho has gone to the house of a much-hated local German and '*cut through his neck so deeply that his whole head fell forward and dangled onto his chest.*' I skim ahead, and doing some pretty swift editorial swerving, manage to cut straight to the jaunty dialogue:

'"*To me you are a great hero,*" *I said.*'

'Why? Why is he, Mummy?'

'Er, he's killed a German. A German baddie.'

'Is he a Nazi?'

They've seen Nazis in *Raiders of the Lost Ark*, another dubious choice on my part, as the phone rang when the baddies' faces melted and I failed to fast-forward in time.

'He's a *German Nazi*,' explains Lawrence wearily to his sister.

'I know how to kill Nazis!' says Lydia helpfully. 'You buy a bagel, and cut it in half and put foxglove seeds all round the circle, then they die.'

And they go to sleep, comforted by thoughts of Nazis eating Jewish snacks laced with digitalis.

When I put the book back, I notice Catherine Storr's *Marianne Dreams*, the dark, post-Freudian novella about a girl stuck in bed with flu on her tenth birthday who draws a house which in her sleep becomes real. There are stones all around it which in the dreams grow tall and menacing. She meets a boy in the house and when they both become trapped by the stones – *which now have eyes* – they have to try and escape. '*Phallic symbols, of course*,' said my mother, which luckily didn't spoil it for me. When I first read it over thirty years ago, it scared the living shit out of me. Suitable for ages four and five? Well, they can always sleep with the light on. Someone else will have to read it to them, though.

In the middle of the night, Peter says: 'Keep still! What are you doing?'

In vain I am changing position, thinking of the head dangling on the chest.

20 Don't Say Butt, Say *Bum*

At Lawrence's school, the standard of reading is scarily high. But as he's got nothing to compare it with, he seems not to notice. He has to do ten minutes at home every night, which makes a welcome alternative to fighting with Lydia. He's moved up to Year 1, where instead of the cuddly-cosy Nursery, he's in a labyrinthine jumble of buildings, and a regime of lining up in the playground behind his teacher at the start of the day. Parents may not come into the classrooms. If I wait to watch him line up, I get a lump in my throat so I leave before. But if he's not actually playing with anyone I get a lump in my throat as well, so I have to wait until he is – or try and put him together with another boy so I can leave without breaking into tears.

At home time we queue outside. One day I get there to be greeted by his new teacher, with a face like doom, saying that Lawrence has left his toy in the Wrong Place. They are allowed to bring a small toy – not a

Game Boy, not a guided missile – and named. They recommend a tennis ball, the one thing we mothers don't give them because of its tendency to bounce over the wall onto the railway line, causing Eurostar drivers to think they're being attacked by miniature versions of Barnes Wallis. Lawrence has brought a Bionicle, the wrong size and unnamed, with a removable – losable – brain. We've played brain transplants with it going up the road.

'I've lost the brain!' he wails. I know how he feels.

'Could Lawrence just look for his brain?' I can't resist asking. She is not amused. Of course, she could be asking herself why she chose a job dealing with six year olds. Personally, I'd rather dig coal.

'It was not in the Toy Tray,' she says, sounding like a Colditz guard who's just found your tunnel. I half expect the next line to be, '*So he's been shot. You may collect the body from the Main Hall. Please ensure it is named.*' We retrieve the brain from its refuge under the radiator, and flee.

Then someone, a parent, complains about Lawrence to the school. He has slapped their child, and they haven't had a quiet word – they've written a *letter*. That's one stop short of legal. The teacher tells me quite kindly. She probably feels a bit sorry for me, lumbered with a psychopath. I am mortified. I tell him off all the way down the road, round the corner and up to the news-agent's. Then it occurs to me to ask him for *his* version.

'Lawrence, did you slap someone?'

'Yes!'

'Who?'

'Pxxx. But he kicked me first!' One down, two to go.

'OK, and did you slap or hit anyone else?'

'Txxx. But he punched me! Just leave me alone, will you?!' But he didn't do it first. OK, well . . . um. I suddenly realize I don't know what my strategy is. Has he been wrongly accused? Should he stand there and take it?

'If anyone's playing too rough, don't hit them back, just – move away from them, OK?'

'OK, Mummy.'

'And if it goes on, tell a teacher.'

'O-*kaaay!*'

'I've got to the bottom of it,' I tell the teacher confidently. 'It was Pxxx and Txxx, and clearly there was silliness on both sides.'

'Ah,' she says. 'I'm afraid the letter wasn't about either of them.'

'You're kidding.' She isn't.

'Look, it was a new boy, one not used to going to school. He probably isn't used to the rough and tumble of the playground.'

'So you're saying the mother over-reacted?'

'A bit, possibly, yes.'

'And you won't tell me who?'

'Sorry.'

How *dare* some over-protective – *twat* – write letters about my child! Right! I bet it's the one who's just moved back here from America – infected, no doubt, by their ludicrous culture of blaming. These are the sort of people who sue God because they think they should be entitled to avoid death. Yes, yes, it must be her! Recently I've noticed that the mother's been a bit stand-offish. She always used to come up and talk to me; now she seems not to see me. Adopting my softly-softly, FBI-on-Valium approach, I ask Lawrence if he's had a fight with her son.

'Oh, yes – we've had about twenty fights.'

'But are you still friends?'

'Nope.'

Right, that's it. He's quite breezy about the whole thing. But I – I, on the other hand – am affronted. How *dare* this woman attack my child – and in print?! In my head I go up to her in the playground, poke her in the chest and ask her just what the bloody hell she thinks she's playing at. We've never had complaints from *anyone*. My son's never been in trouble in his life. If her son can't cope with school, maybe he should stay at home. And she can piss off as well. In a gathering of middle-class mummies in hairbands, I have turned into a hard-faced cow with no tights and a tattoo, smoking and shoving sweets at the baby while threatening an innocent person with actual bodily harm. Well, in my head.

Peter thinks I'm over-reacting.

'Of course I don't like it when someone – I don't even know who it is – complains about me and . . . well, how would you like it?'

'Lawrence.'

'What.'

'They complained about Lawrence, not you.'

'Yeah?! So?'

'It's not happening to you. And anyway, he's fine. Look at him.'

True, he is contentedly running a toy car down a cardboard poster tube. But I am not satisfied. When we next visit Peter's sister, I demand an explanation. She runs a centre for 'impossible' children, for God's sake; she must have the answer!

'I mean, three different boys. What's going on?'

'Boys fight,' she says.

'That's it? That's the entire sum of your thirty years' experience?'

'I'm afraid so.'

'I thought you knew stuff.'

'Not really. I have made sticky chicken, though.'

'And you think that solves everything, do you?'

Peter has his Objective voice on.

'It's good you've married into a family which doesn't panic.'

'Who isn't any *use*.'

'It neutralizes the Calman anxiety quotient.'

He thinks we run about with our arms flailing, emotionally over-reacting to everything all the time, like characters in a bad Italian film, and that his Mission on Earth is to balance us out. I only have to come home with any kind of complaint or problem I've heard in the playground for him to say: 'You haven't heard the Other Side.'

'If I said they were rounding up Jews in Dulwich Village, but that they hadn't rounded me up *personally*, would you say that?'

He gives me his Rising Above It look. You can almost see his feet leave the floor.

'If it wasn't for me you'd be—'

'Crazy or dead, I know. And if it wasn't for *me*, you'd be going on wine-tasting holidays and polishing the car at weekends.'

However, there is an unexpected upside to this shoulder shrugging. In fact, I'm about to appreciate that Balance can be a Good Thing. Having the children at a scarily high-powered school gives us licence to let go at other times. No: we have to, to achieve Balance. Now that Lawrence is being drilled in spelling and times tables all day, I no longer worry about the fact that he lies around all weekend eating Quavers and watching Jackie Chan. In fact, I insist upon it. Peter thinks long and hard before giving me his analysis.

'Our children need to watch more television,' he says.

Not everyone shares this view. In fact, if there's one thing that unites the middle classes – far more firmly than food or politics – it's the attitude to television. Even mothers who use formula milk agree that TV is Bad. Whenever I take mine to someone else's house, the first thing they do – if they're a woman, obviously – is apologize for the mess. (Men don't do this. Left alone with children for any length of time, they don't tidy; they're triumphant if the house doesn't burn down.) Then, if the television is on, they leap up, look at it as if they've never seen it before, and rush to switch it off, saying, '*I just put it on for a few minutes while I was boiling*

the kettle/answering the phone/having 4.5 seconds to myself.'
Then, they have to add: *'They hardly ever watch it.'*

Why? Because they have to prove what good mothers
they are. Letting our children watch television is like
masturbation used to be. We all do it. We're pretty sure
– no, we *know* – everyone else does, yet we feel guilty
about it. Nonetheless, we can't stop doing it. And as with
household mess, the more we hide it, the worse other
women feel when *they* do it, and so on. Why?

Aha, you see. Television's bad because (a) it gives
mothers a break, and (b) it's *passive*. You sit down, and
. . . you don't have to make notes, or draw or build
anything out of Lego while you watch, so . . . Hang on,
isn't that just like going to the cinema? Only – er,
cheaper? Is *that* bad? If you go to your local UGC or Vue,
or whatever it's called now, and you suddenly see your
friends going past, do you have to rush and hide behind
a cut-out of Tom Hanks? And if they spot you, do you
have to say, *'Honestly, we hardly ever go. Actually, we were
looking for the library and came in here by mistake?'*

And while we're at it, what about other passive
activities? If you go to the opera and sit still in your seat,
just listening – assuming you're not one of those people
who follow the score which you carry around in a black
velvet pouch – is *that* passive? If you stand in front of a

painting in a gallery and just look at it – don't write a thesis or ski at the same time – is *that* passive? If you go underneath during sex, is *that*? Sex is the original inter- active entertainment you could say, but one of the things that's always drawn me to it is that it's one of the few exercises you – generally – do lying down. But is it less passive, and therefore better, if you go on top? (In the seventies there were books for wimmin that said it was.) And if you read a book at the same time, is that best of all? More educational? More middle class? There's a character in Martin Scorsese's *Alice Doesn't Live Here Anymore*, a waitress, who's always sparring with her boss the chef. Alice, the polite new girl, thinks she hates him. Then the waitress suddenly yells right across the kitchen: 'Mel, I could lie under you, eat fried chicken and do a crossword puzzle – all at the same time!'

Now, that's multi-tasking. But back to television.

My mother, while not accusing me openly, is very fond of the phrase, *The Electronic Nanny*. She groups it with other supposedly down-market maternal failings, such as smoking, bottle feeding and not talking to kids when they are small. I'm not going to be drawn into a contest about who has the more intellectual values, so let me just say that this is a bit rich, coming from someone who has been known to watch *Shoestring*. She brought us up on *loads* of telly, which is particularly bad when you consider that when I was small, it was only on for about five hours a day. In those days, nice kids only watched about eight minutes. A week.

And no wonder: most of it was crap. There was *Watch With Mother*, with *Andy Pandy* on Tuesday, *Bill and Ben* on Wednesday and so on, for about twenty incredibly bland minutes, and only really two programmes for the five-plus age, which were *Jackanory* – not bad, depending on the story – and *Blue Peter*. Thank God we were never made to watch that. It was full of hearty types collecting milk bottle tops, going on about 'targets' represented for some reason by giant thermometers, and endlessly stroking animals – something both my parents regarded as tedious and faintly suspect, like the Scouts. As we got older though, the choice improved: we had *Dr Who*, *Star Trek*, *Lost in Space*, *Voyage to the Bottom of the Sea*, *The Avengers* and *The Prisoner*, often as we ate supper. And – get this – the TV was even *on the table*.

Now we have some very good television. Of course, that brings different challenges. The children have been put in front of *The Simpsons* as soon as they could sit up. But I'm not very keen on the word 'butt'. However my attempts to try and weed it out of their vocabulary fail completely.

'Lawrence. Don't say butt: say "bum".'
'OK, Bum-head!'

I've got no one to blame but myself, so it's a relief to know that as they get older, their peer group will become more significant. We take a keen interest in Lawrence and Lydia's classmates. As I've said, we're looking for charming and well-off children who'll invite them on lavish holidays. But also, when things go pear-shaped, we'll need someone to blame. When I was fourteen, the two poshest girls in my class were arrested outside Lords cricket ground – in their nighties – attempting to steal a *Members Only* sign with a pair of wire-cutters. In the aftermath, the main thing both sets of parents were concerned with was blaming the other girl. So your child's best friend is yours too. Possibly.

Lawrence has already fallen under the spell of one boy who he wanted to impress by doing naughty things. At three, the scope of their naughtiness was fairly limited. Splashing water on the cloakroom floor is something even private schools don't get *too* heated about. But two years on, the horizons are widening fast. Lawrence is now very keen on another sinisterly charismatic boy who has a talent for bringing out the worst in people, a bit like some TV producers. When he comes round to play after school one day, I think, as you do: *They've gone very quiet* . . . Then I get upstairs to find lists of expletives – including the c-word – neatly written out and taped to the bedroom wall. Should I use Positive Reinforcement? Say: 'That's *very* good writing, boys. Perhaps a different list of words now?' Or a more Andrea Dworkin-style response comes to mind: 'I feel abused by your use of a name for the female genitalia to promote the wholesale degradation of women. This word makes me feel violated.'

But though I'm not fond of the c-word, my primal fear is of the reaction from other parents. I don't want it there when one of Lydia's well-brought-up little friends comes round. They won't even recognize it, I shouldn't think, but their mothers will shun me as the Amish would have Kelly McGillis, had she slept with Harrison Ford in *Witness*. And while I'd risk a bit of shunning for a night with Harrison, I'm not prepared to go under socially for the sake of a word.

While I'm considering this, I voice my immediate concern: 'What have I told you about Sellotape? You've bloody well gone and taken the paint off the wall! Look!'

While taking it off I do mutter something about people finding the c-word upsetting, and insist that next time they use Blu-Tack. It's a bit like under-age sex, I suppose: you don't want them to be doing it at all, but if they *are* doing it, could they at least use a condom?

Shortly after this, I see the boy who taught them the c-word ringing old ladies' doorbells and running away – something I and my friends did a lot at that age. And the warm glow of satisfaction that comes from seeing a child behave worse than mine makes everything in the world right again.

But the *status*, does not remain, as it were, *quo*. Rude words, like the spores of GM crops, are in the air and drifting towards us. If we want to keep our children pristine, we should have started off like the family at my sister's school, who allowed no outside influences whatsoever, even to the point of birthday parties with no guests. But anyhow their plan backfired: they mistook my mother's erudite aura for mental purity, and allowed them to mix with *us*.

So as we observe the intellectual contamination of our children, the rather disconcerting reality becoming apparent is that *we* are the bad influence. It takes a bit of getting used to. In fact, a touch of chemical comfort is required. One night, quite pissed, I go up to their room to find out what the loud thumping is. When I come in, they are bouncing on their beds, shouting: '*Shit, pooh, fucking hell!*'

It has a catchy kind of rhythm. I find myself joining in. Peter comes up and joins in as well. We agree that it is the funniest thing we have ever heard.

But of course we never hear it again, because I have – accidentally – invoked Newton's Third Law of Parenting, which is that you have only to join in an activity for your children to reject it immediately. Right: that's the smoking issue solved. I may get lung cancer, but it'll be worth it.

Well, actually that's not quite true. The real reason we haven't heard '*Shit, pooh, fucking hell!*' again is that they've found something else to frighten us with and this time I really don't have anyone else to blame. Just before Lydia's sixth birthday, two brothers the same age as her and Lawrence come round to play. I suggest some music with their supper, and Lydia chooses Michael Jackson.

Now, I see no reason to deprive my kids of some great pop music, just because of an artist's preposterous, creepy, and quite probably sinister personal life. But I am reckoning without their excellent memories. I mean, it must be ages since they asked me why he'd been arrested, and I tried to – well, answer honestly. But, my mind being full of vital matters such as swimming kits and running out of ketchup, I don't remember. So here is the exchange I overhear during the meal:

LYDIA, putting on *Thriller*: 'Michael Jackson got

arrested. But this was before he got arrested. (The junior equivalent of describing it as Middle Period Michael Jackson.) He wasn't a robber or anything.'

FRIEND, aged seven: 'What did he do?'

LYDIA, casually: 'He slept in a child's bed.' Friend looks baffled.

LAWRENCE, knowledgeably: 'If the adult doesn't know the child, and sleeps in the child's bed, that's against the law.' Friend is even more baffled. Friend's little brother, aged five, is sitting over his shepherd's pie with eyes like LPs. My son then goes on to detail how to entrap an unfavourite adult.

'Say there's a grown-up you don't like much. You just invite them for a sleepover and when they're in your bed you just call the police! Can we have pudding now, Mummy?'

21 Stabbed *and* Picked On

Some time has gone by since they've been to the dentist. They went once, to a nice man called Dennis, ran round and round his surgery until the nurse had to contain them, and got stickers. Then no reminders arrived, so I left it. There's a mother at school who's a dentist, but just knowing one doesn't count. I think about it, open the address book to 'Dentist', and leave it for a few months. Eventually Lawrence starts complaining of a pain on his upper left side. On the way to school I notice a nearer dentist, in a sweet little house. We could save forty minutes' driving time. It's private, but the charge for a check-up isn't too bad. I make an appointment. The receptionist is very nice. The waiting room has a piano. A sign says: *Please feel free to play the piano.* I tell the children: 'Stay away from that.'

The dentist puts Lawrence in the chair and tells Lydia where to stand. Exactly where. Possibly she has had a bad experience with a child lunging forward, tripping, and making her stab a patient with one of those sharp prongy things. Or she could be one of those people who has to tell people where to stand.

'Stay there,' I say to Lydia. She moves her foot. 'No, *there*.' The slightest movement might provoke this woman to do God knows what.

'So – you want me to do something about this hole.'

'Hole . . .?'

'Two, actually, I'm afraid.'

'*Two??*' Play for time. What do politicians do? Talk about something else. 'The – er, well, of course I've – Lydia! Stay still!'

'I assume you've seen it while cleaning his teeth?'

'Er. Well . . . Lydia! Don't move!'

'You look shocked.'

'Well, of course! It's not as though he hasn't been brushing. He doesn't even have that many sweets. They both do. Don't. *Lydia!*'

I am humiliated. My mother was obsessed with teeth. She grew up in pre-war Glasgow where her dentist was an alcoholic and the diet was terrible; many people had to wait for the NHS to be created so they could get their first full set of teeth. She wouldn't buy, or let us have, Coke, squash, fizzy drinks, ice lollies or boiled sweets, because of the oral carnage she had witnessed in her formative years. Now, my pristine son has got holes in him. I can't tell her. We'll have to move, disappear into the Bad Mothers Protection Programme.

'And when we do the procedure, we find it's much better if you don't stay.'

Hang on a minute . . .

'We find the anxiety transmits itself to the child and generally makes it worse.' Anxiety? What anxiety? I'm not anxious, I'm *ashamed*. This is another test and I have failed.

'Are you good at times tables, Lawrence?' Lawrence looks doubtful. He must be wondering, as I am, what the hell they have to do with teeth. 'We always do times tables when we do fillings. We have lots of fun.'

He looks aghast. She invites him to get down, and I assume it is safe for Lydia to move. As we reach the door, she says: 'Oh, and make sure your shoes are clean next time, will you?'

I'm too stunned to answer. We get out of there, and all I can hear in my head is, *Your son has dirty shoes.* When I get him to school: 'Bye-bye! See you at home time!' *Your son has dirty shoes.* In the supermarket: 'Buy One, Get One Free!' *Your son has dirty shoes.* In the car, listening to the radio: 'Come on, Minister, answer the question.' *Your son has dirty shoes.* It's like *King Midas and the Ass's Ears*, in which the foolish king is punished by Apollo for judging his music not to be the sweetest. The barber who sees the king's deformity is driven mad by the burden of his secret and shouts it into the grass. The grass grows and the secret is whispered on the wind continuously – until the whole world knows. Somehow, everything I've achieved as a mother feels undermined by this slur. True, they're not the cleanest children in the world, but I am – in my own bumbling way – proud of them. I can't get over this – judgement.

At some point, my mother rings.

'How are things?'

'I took Lawrence to a scary dentist who said he had lots of holes and had to do times tables and clean his shoes. I hardly give them any sweets. They *do* brush their teeth, they really do! I'm sorry, I'm sorry!'

'Oh, dear! Well, I'm sure there's another dentist he can see.'

There is. There is Dennis. His practice is not in a sweet little house. It is on a frightening main road flanked by Exhaust Centres and House Clearance shops. There is no piano in the waiting room, only a man humming.

'And when was his last visit?'

The receptionist makes me feel better: bleached blonde and motherly, with a smoky voice that suggests a lot of nightlife in the past.

'Um . . .' I don't mention our defection. 'It could have been a while.'

'I'll just check . . .'

I start tensing up. She's going to judge me. No, come on! Claire had a boyfriend who didn't go for twelve years. Maybe it's not as long as I thought. Time flies when you—

'Here we are. Ooh, it's been two years!'

Christ! No wonder he's got two holes. His whole head's rotting away and it's my fault.

'We didn't get a reminder. I hardly ever give them sweets. He has been brushing.'

Dennis says: 'We haven't seen you for a while.'

'We didn't get a reminder.'

'Well, let's have a look.'

Lawrence squirms a bit.

'Sit still, Lawrence, for God's sake!'

That's a good technique: take out your guilt about not taking them to the dentist's by snapping at them when you do get there.

'Oh. Hm. Ah.'

'What?'

'Presumably you've seen this hole?'

275

I choose my words carefully.

'I am aware of it, yes. Lydia, get away from there.'

'I mean, the one nearer the front is much smaller, but—'

'There *are* two, then. God . . .' My hope that there are no holes, that the other dentist is mad, fizzles out. Why didn't we get one of those little white cards? If he'd bothered to send reminders, we wouldn't be in this mess.

'Yes. You see – can you lean back again, Lawrence? The smaller one's there. And the rather larger one is . . . *there*.'

I can see it now. Almost half the tooth is gone. I feel weak.

'I don't understand it. He has been brushing. They both have, and she's fine. Lydia, stop skipping.'

'Well, nonetheless . . .'

'I don't know what to say.' In the periphery of my vision I can see a needle. In my anxiety to disprove neglect, I completely ignore Lawrence. I don't care what he's feeling, only what Dennis thinks of *me*. His hand moves towards the needle.

'Shall we put that side to sleep?' I wish I could. Now I have to reassure my poor little boy by hiding my fear of needles. I must try to remember not to widen my eyes when he picks it up and brandishes it in the air. Breathe slowly. Keep focusing on him, not the hypo . . . So far, so good . . .

'Oooh!' says Lydia. 'What a *big needle!*'

'Lydia, go out to reception and get one of those books you were looking at.'

'I don't want to.'

'Go on!'

'No!'

Luckily, this has slightly diverted Lawrence's attention and the needle is now in. But it stays in, of course, for ages. He groans.

'Try not to move,' says Dennis. Time slows down. He has had that needle in his cheek forever. After about a century it comes out.

'Well done!' I say. 'The worst is over.'

But when he attempts to do the filling, Dennis discovers the area is not numb. He has to do the whole thing again.

'I don't like to give them too much . . .' he muses. But on the other hand, my child seems to have the constitution of a mammoth. He ends up with virtually an adult dose. And even then, he is so resistant that Dennis can't manage the second filling at all.

'It's starting to wear off. I don't think I'd better attempt the second one. We'll do it when you come back.'

'Come back?' The filling is temporary. We have to do

it all again. I take him to the toy shop and buy him a glow-in-the-dark set of Geomag for £10.99. He has already has a non-glow-in-the-dark set that lives under the bed, and after one play, this one joins it there.

When we come back, again Lawrence needs not one, but two, long stabs with the needle. Throughout it all he is incredibly quiet, sweet and good. Despite this, I berate him for not doing his teeth properly. Not surprisingly, he wants some kind of compensation for being stabbed *and* picked on, all in the one day.

'Ice cream?!' I splutter. 'You've just had a filling!!' So, feeling even worse, I buy him the Mousetrap game for £22.99. He and Lydia open it all over the floor and immediately lose several of the pieces. But I feel ever so slightly better.

22 Sex in the Ad Break of *Friends*

Now that Lydia and Lawrence are showing an interest in the subject – examining each other in the bath, giggling, etc. – it seems the right time to share with them the Great Wonder of the Miracle of Life. I have planned how it will go. There'll be no cutesy stuff, but it won't just be dry science either. They'll sit at my knee, their little faces gazing up in wonderment, as I – like David Attenborough – impart this Great Truth.

'Gosh!' they will gasp.

And: 'Wow!'

Possibly followed by: '*Urgh!*'

But that's fine, because I am expecting it. I am Not Embarrassed, and everything is under control.

When's the Right Time? Some people are still shirking the issue when their kids are pushing puberty. A bit late; you don't want to leave it until they know more than you. So I decide to go for the point where they're old enough to understand the basics, but not too old to think that willies and so on are inherently fascinating. I shall not shirk! For once, I am going to copy my mother.

I was five when she began her comprehensive run-down of the Facts of Life. This was in the Sixties, when a lot of kids believed that babies came from the huge bottles of coloured liquid that stood in the windows of chemists'. God knows why; it was just accepted in many quarters, like having Dream Topping instead of cream, and wearing a vest. Looking back, quite a few of the parents probably believed it as well. Mum would have none of it. Having drawn the pictures for various public health leaflets with titles like *You and Your Breasts* she was fearless and tireless. She gave us the full itinerary of the sperm – including the fate of stragglers, diversions and blocked fallopian tubes, and the entire life cycle of the ovum, from ovulation through menstruation in all its glory, to conception and beyond. From erections and secretions she did not flinch. The only problem was getting her to stop. By eleven I was running from the room, begging: 'Can I do my maths homework now? *Please?*'

It was like *Star Wars*; just when you thought you'd heard the last of it, along came yet another bit of the story you were sure you didn't need. On the other hand, it served me well at secondary school. Friends came round eagerly, knowing that my mum would answer all the questions theirs wouldn't. She also let me read *The ABZ of Love*, with its – shall we say – generously illustrated entry on 'erection'. While bunking off games, a few of us would gather in the cloakroom to discuss it all – very useful, as at fourteen, the range of experience was wide. One girl was in a grown-up relationship – *'last night we did 69'* said one of her notes passed along the back row in Latin, while another was a strict Catholic whose mother described sex as, *'something terrible you have to do when you get married'*. She'd obviously got it mixed up with ironing. Relying on the biology syllabus was not recommended; thanks to the poor quality of early photocopying, in the mock O level the male and female reproductive systems looked the same. One of my friends labelled the male one as the female, so you can't assume anything. During my period not long ago, I tried to explain to Lydia about ovaries; I told her: *'You've got all your eggs already, in two little boxes in your tummy,'* to which she replied: *'Are there chicks in there?'*

So I am primed. But as usual, events get ahead of me.

Watching *Friends* one night, I become aware of the patter of tiny hands and knees. They have snuck in and are arranging themselves, like decorative bolsters, along the back of the sofa. Peter is out, so I grab the chance to curry favour.

'I'm going to be really nice and let you watch for a bit, OK?'

They ignore me. They are already deep into Rachel's intention to say goodbye to Barry the Dentist.

It's an old episode. Once upon a time, in the past, Rachel was going to marry Barry, but she called it off. Now she's been seeing him again, but he's about to marry her friend Mindy and she does, like, have a conscience y'know. So she goes to his surgery to say she can't see him any more. And they end up having sex in the chair. The sex itself being just implied – this is network after all, not HBO – the children initially only have Rachel's encoded references to go on.

When Phoebe and Monica ask: *'So, did you go see Barry?'* she says: *'Ye-es . . .'*

'How did he take it?' says Monica. And Rachel answers (Big Laugh here): *'. . . Quite well!'*

Then Monica says, *'You have dental floss in your hair.'* (Another Big Laugh.) This of course goes right over their heads. However, her confession grips them immediately.

'They had sex in the dental chair! They had sex in the dental chair!' they chant, bouncing the poor old sofa to hell. And I suddenly realize that they have no idea what 'sex' actually is. For all they know it could be root canal work. There's going to be no David Attenborough Moment. I have to tell them now.

'Kids, shall I tell you what sex is?'

'Sssh!'

'Mummy, *move*! I can't see!'

I bide my time and wait for the break.

I must focus. I've got approximately two minutes. The *Friends* bumper comes up.

'OK, listen. Sex is when a man and a lady love each other and do lots of kissing, and the man puts his willy into the lady's *noo-noo*.' They are hysterical at the idea, not least because it's only recently that they've started becoming helpless at the word *noo-noo*, although we've used it for ages.

With about fifteen seconds left I don't go into more detail, but do add, having seen them eyeing each other speculatively: 'Only grown-ups are allowed to do it.'

Friends comes back on. In the rush to describe the whole procedure, I have forgotten to mention it can make a baby.

23 Party Bag

Lawrence is about to be seven. People say you should avoid having an August baby, but they're wrong. Because their birthday always falls in the holidays, you never have to have a party with thirty kids. Or twenty. Or even ten. In fact, because *almost the whole class is away* at this time, numbers are extremely low. This year, we are taking Lawrence and two friends to the zoo. With Lydia that makes four. And the timing is perfect, because this very month, Komodo Dragons have arrived – 'launched', if that's the right word, by David Attenborough. Attenborough is Lawrence's hero. He is getting three entire series of his programmes for a birthday present, adding up to about 4,000 hours of viewing. I figure if we put the first disc on now, he'll be switching off about March.

When we get to the zoo, it turns out that launched is exactly the right word, as, a week before our arrival, one of the Dragons leaps off a wall and ends up in hospital. That leaves one other, which when we visit has under-

284

standably succumbed to agoraphobia, and a much smaller – presumably infant – example, which loiters disconsolately among the municipal, *Ground Force*-style landscaping.

But it's fine because there are birds – Lawrence's favourite – and the aquarium, which is still 'undeveloped', i.e. the animals haven't been replaced by corporate-sponsored video screens. It is exactly as it was when I last came thirty years ago. And the children get a first-hand idea of what it's like to actually live underwater, since the rain is coming through the ceiling. Afterwards, we have lunch out. It's not expensive, yet, with the entrance tickets and snacks, we seem to have spent £200. We go back on the tube, exhausted. But at least we've saved the £200 we would otherwise have spent on an entertainer and a church hall. And we have managed to tire them out by accidentally booking a restaurant nowhere near the zoo.

Two months later, Lydia is six. Her party will be making palaces out of cardboard boxes with me and Katarina, so she is allowed only five guests because – and this is an important point – *'you can't make palaces with more than six'*. Unfortunately, in the run-up to her birthday I lose the list, and because my memory doesn't extend to six names, tell one of the mothers who's trying to lift share that the child she wants to share with hasn't been invited, so not to mention it. But she has been. The confusion spreads until – none of the other five wanting to say the wrong thing – the poor woman wonders why every time she suggests a lift share they all change the subject. On the day, I find the list at the bottom of a huge pile of papers, and manage not to upset any six year olds – just. But to be fair to me, I have a lot on my plate – literally.

We are supposed to be decorating the sitting room as the underwater kingdom of the Sea-Fairy Queen, the autocratic mermaid I invented at the seaside. But a week before, our DVD club accidentally sends us *The Belstone Fox*, a rather dark 1973 film starring Eric Porter – and Dennis Waterman, on horseback – which opens with a family of foxes being battered to death with spades. One cub survives ('Tag') and is rescued, to be brought up with the very hounds being trained to exterminate it on the hunt. At the end, Tag manages to get most of the hounds killed by leading them onto the railway track, and Eric Porter dies in a cave. Lydia loves it, and skips about telling anyone within a three-mile radius incomprehensible chunks of the plot. And she doesn't want the underwater kingdom any more, she wants this. Peter has also bought her a cuddly fox from Ikea from which she is now inseparable, so this is partly his fault. I phone him.

'Forget the Sea-Fairy Queen; we've got to do a country landscape with fox and hounds.'

'But I've just got all this green netting.'

'She doesn't want it.'

'Well, can't you persuade her?'

'Hey, here's an idea! If you don't want her to become obsessed with foxes, don't take her to Ikea and buy her a bloody great big one.'

'You didn't complain at the time.'

'I forgot.'

I too am disappointed. I've been looking forward to suspending the green netting below the ceiling and hanging twirly green crepe paper from it for seaweed. I was going to put little boats on it, and stick a couple of Barbies up there, swimming, with their legs hanging down so when you look up it's like those underwater shots in *Jaws*. I really wanted – oh, never mind. Lydia is only interested in the fox story, and won't go anywhere without 'Tag'. It has to sit on the table while she eats her cereal, where it attracts abuse from Lawrence and becomes spattered with Weetabix and Pritt Stick.

'Do you like *The Belstone Fox*, Mummy?'

'Yes, it's very good.'

'I'm going to have it on my cake!'

'Ah. Right . . .'

I ring my friend Judith, who rashly once mentioned that she is a serious cake decorator.

'How's it going?'

'Er – fine. You know Lydia's birthday?'

'How's the underwater scene going?'

'We-ell . . . I give her the outline of *The Belstone Fox*, leaving out the bit where Eric Porter dies in the cave.

'What's this got to do with it?'

'She wants the whole thing on top of her cake.'

'What?!'

'You haven't got any tips, have you?' If she lived nearer, I'd pop round and get a quick masterclass, but she's on the other side of London, so all I can do is moan.

'Actually,' she says after some thought, 'I'm not doing anything tonight. I'll make you one.'

'What?!'

'A fox in sugar paste. How big d'you want it? Roughly.'

The next day I get two trains and a bus to meet her outside Hamley's, where she is waiting with a plastic box. I open it and, sure enough, inside is an amazingly accurate representation of a fox. I carry it home carefully, like Mike Hammer with the plutonium in *Kiss Me*

Deadly, and in the remaining hour before school ends, make a cub.

The image in my head is surprisingly hard to translate into marzipan. The head and body don't want to stick together, and to get the orangey-brown right I have to use a lot of black, red and yellow colouring which end up all over the kitchen counter and my hands. Also, it won't stand up. So I lie it down on the white icing. It looks like a turd with a tail, but I figure if I position it near the other one it'll get the benefit of the doubt. Anyhow, Lydia will definitely appreciate that I've opened every single shoebox in the attic to find my old dolls' house garden spade to lean against the Matchmaker fence.

'Look! That's the spade the farmers use to beat the foxes to death!'

'Oh, thank you so much, Mummy!'

The Matchmaker fence is the *pièce de résistance*. It takes me about an hour the night before, snapping off lengths that aren't quite the same, eating them and snapping off some more, followed by dabbing very, very small amounts of chocolate icing on the ends and holding them together, and then when that doesn't work, getting involved with golden syrup. In the end I manage only one section of two-bar fence, which is grabbed off the cake and eaten by another child before anyone sees it properly. But Lydia loves her cake, so I can die happy.

We just have to do a few games first. My mother did wonderful games. She even always had a spare prize tucked behind the record player for the little brother or sister who'd burst into tears because they hadn't won, usually because they hadn't actually played. So I'm buoyed along by a warm current of nostalgia. I'll do Pass the Parcel because it means the children sitting down for a while, I can remember how to play it, and I like wrapping things. I dig out the set of pencils someone gave Lydia last year and surround myself with the Arts section of the Sunday paper. As I go along I read the odd paragraph, then, with time ticking on a bit too briskly, I just slap the pages on and stuff the pleasingly fat, finished item behind the kettle. Several hours later, I discover the downside of using the Books section, when the game stops abruptly, despite the strains of *Beat It* continuing to throb through the walls. Now I think of it, I do vaguely remember the name *Pol Pot* flashing past, but didn't think much of it. I gather up the discarded pages more efficiently than usual.

'Why are there skulls on the wrapping paper?' asks one of the girls.

'Er, just shove it in the bag would you?'

Party Bag

The brother of one of them, who's seeing an educational psychologist, thinks it's 'cool'.

We send the kids away with their cardboard palaces, and their parents are all nice enough to look grateful for going-home presents which are basically decorated litter.

24 Nature v Nurture:
Pink Blizzards and the Great Escape

Something rather serious has happened, something that won't surprise anyone with children older than ours; it's just shocked me, that's all. Lydia has recently turned six. Lawrence is still seven. And their father has announced that he is taking Lawrence to see the *Great Escape* exhibition at the Imperial War Museum, *and not Lydia*. What are she and I doing instead? Going to John Lewis to buy *Velcro*.

I know what this means. It's the beginning of Lydia's becoming a *girl*. In his eyes, she has joined the ranks of people who wear pink and mince about in tutus and – evidently from his decision re this weekend's outing – are not interested in the Second World War. So let me just say that as a female who has sat through more documentaries on Colditz, the SOE and Churchill than the entire male population of NATO, I feel a little short-changed. I mean, surely one of the rewards for long service in front of flickering Lancaster bombers and chaps giving Jerry a blasting should be the chance to climb through Tom, Dick and Harry and buy a medal in the museum shop afterwards. And if Lydia wants to come too, who is he to stop her? But she doesn't. And I feel a bit sad.

Up until now we've been comrades, a gang of four, sharing the same interests. Well, more or less. Peter can't watch a subtitled film without moaning about it, and doesn't know the difference between Katherine Mansfield and Jayne Mansfield. (He was impressed that a busty film star had managed to write short stories and knew H. G. Wells.) And I've forgotten the names of the five father and son Formula One racing drivers I memorized for the wedding. But on the whole, we all paddle the same canoe. We all built towers together and helicopter landing pads when they were little; they both still make dens behind the sofa – which is *unisex* – to use a word from my youth, but there is an overall bias towards the masculine. Lydia has grown up with boys' toys – not because we despise all things feminine, but because Peter, Lawrence and I all like them and we were here first. When she came along we already had the toy garage from Peter's nephews, hundreds of cars, Scalextric (my wedding present to him) and, thanks to various neighbours, a plastic castle and Sherwood Forest set, plus double our combined weight in Lego. And with most of the junior videos – *Bob the Builder, Fireman Sam, Thomas,* etc. – being so blokeish, the household bias was male. But this is mitigated by Lawrence's nurturing side; dressing-up clothes are much used by both, and the dolls' beds two Christmases ago were more popular with Lawrence. He went through a phase of parenting a teddy called John Calman, followed by a tortoise and an elephant, '*both eight years old, Mummy: they're twins.*'

But Lawrence has, I reckon, more room for manoeuvre. Ever since I had Lydia, I've been amazed by how society's ancient attitude to females periodically breaks through: '*A girl? Ooh, no thank you. I prefer boys. Boys are simpler. Girls are spiteful. You know where you are with boys.*' And so on, from people you can't somehow imagine saying, '*Oh, your husband's black: they're stupid and lazy.*'

At the park, Peter and I watch Lydia climb trees in a tiara, and give ourselves credit for producing a truly modern daughter.

Still, I watch for the signs of coyness and excess pink that everyone tells me are coming, even though she is by no means as 'girly' as most of her friends. My own dolls' house, made out of hardboard forty years ago and in need of extensive refurbishment, provokes not so much as a peep of curiosity. It sits on a shelf in the spare room, with its long-untouched beds, cooker, piano, clock and

six-keyed typewriter made by ten-year-old me out of clay.
Remembering my own longing for a Sindy when I was
given a chemistry set, I come home intermittently with
a doll, fairy, or glittery bracelet. The jewellery is fallen
upon hungrily, but the dolls are generally found at the
bottom of toy pile-ups, limbs twisted and faces horribly
tattooed with pen, like a Friday night in A&E.

So I think that my daughter isn't interested in dolls,
but I am wrong.

Around her fifth birthday, the blizzard of pink starts
falling upon us. We watch helplessly, like extras in a CGI
blockbuster, as it drifts through the windows and trans-
forms the landscape. We know we're powerless to resist.
But that's fine, because I know she can be both: gorgeous
and dynamic; model *and* detective. I get her a Barbie
stamper set – 'it encourages drawing' – and an air
stewardess Sindy, though I call her 'Travel Sindy', to
make her sound like an explorer. We have our first
shopping day together, buy her a dress and pink glittery
tights and have lunch and feel like best friends. Then we
come home and all watch *Die Another Day* together, and
Lydia wants to be Jinx, the sexy and fearless CIA opera-
tive played by Halle Berry. So *that's* OK. I am so relaxed

about the whole thing I even let her have the fluffy unicorn she wants from the pointless shop at the end of the road. Then I begin to notice *signs*.

She fidgets through *Master and Commander* – our favourite film of 2003. Sailors, cannons, cellos – what's not to like? She wants, and gets, a *My Little Pony*, then another – from someone at school who doesn't know we've told her the 'different' ones are pictures of the same one in different colours, and that *'Collect the entire range'* is in fact Korean for *'There is only one'*. She adores *The Lion King* more than ever, and still refers frequently to *Kiara*, which was briefly amusing because at first her father and I thought she was a new girl at school. They say you should watch what your children watch, and they're right. Prolonged viewing of films in which Life's Great Themes are explored by animated wildlife is inspiring her to blab snippets of platitudinous sentiment suited to a low-grade sales course.

After a battle to get her to do her teeth one night she skips away, gushing: 'Thanks, Mum! I'll always believe in you!'

And at bedtime she adds: 'I love you more than Life Itself.' And when I look a touch sceptical, admits: 'I got that from *Robin Hood.*'

And I defend my scepticism, as I suspect that what looks on the outside like concern for the Diversity of Life

296

and our fellow creatures – though mainly those called
Kiara – is actually part of a wider trend towards cutesi-
ness. When she gets something in her eye – a bit of
vinegary chip if you must know – I say: 'Try and cry it
out.'

Lawrence advises: 'Think of something sad.'

And Lydia says: 'I'm thinking of a pencil that hasn't
been sharpened.'

'No!' he says: 'DYING!'

I think that illustrates the difference between the
sexes as well as anything.

And while I am discussing with Peter a Woman's
Right Not to Spend Her Saturday Buying Velcro While
the Menfolk Crawl Through Tunnels and Buy Medals at
the Imperial War Museum, Lydia is packing her ballet
kit for classes she doesn't have.

I have, as usual, brought this on myself.

Strike one! I have got her an *Angelina Ballerina* book,
even though it contains one of my least favourite literary
phenomena, clothed mice. Strike two! A boy at school – I
know *your* game, sonny – gives her an Angelina backpack.
Strike three! I allow Katarina to get her a ballet outfit
for her sixth birthday.

And yet – with my head up my arse in the time-
honoured parental manner – I am hoping the Ballet
Thing might go away. It's not so much ballet I object to

as the culture that surrounds it. I'm sure that the other mothers sign their girls up because they Look Sweet – not a crime in itself, admittedly, but then they don't take their sons to football because they like the strip. I don't want her to aspire to be *decorative*. I want my daughter to stand apart, to plough her own furrow, rev her own – speedboat. So I talk her into doing karate. I've told her it's *like* ballet, but with more jumping. And after six weeks of it, she seems content.

But when we return from our Velcro expedition, she leans the Angelina backpack against the wall by the door and says meekly: 'I'll keep it here in case you decide to let me do ballet.'

And so I go into the kitchen and stab myself with a fork. Naturally, I'm a hypocrite. Of course I did ballet when I was that age. I was forever gazing through the window of *Annello & Davide* at the pointe shoes, and was never without my copy of *Ballet Shoes*, which I regarded as a sort of life manual, the way people these days look upon *Atkins* or *The Purpose-Driven Life*.

But what about Lydia? What about *her* wishes? She wants to do ballet, so shouldn't I just give in? Ah, but! She also wants to be a lion cub, a baby eagle, and – intermittently – a Dalmatian. And while I've given her milk in a saucer on several occasions, I object to dragging her up the road on a string.

Nature v Nurture: Pink Blizzards and the Great Escape

And while all this has been swirling round in my head, the fog clears a little, and a brief exchange with her makes me realize what I *really* want out of all this. However she evolves, I just want to be part of it. And learning that I've already missed one key stage of her development as a woman has made me not want to miss out – on anything. Shortly after not going to *The Great Escape*, I get them Smarties as a treat.

'Hey, Lydia,' I say. 'If you lick the red one and put it on your lips, it makes lipstick!' And she says: 'I *know*.'

Somehow she has managed to experience this without me. But with whom? Where? When? Making lipstick with a red Smartie is a special moment in a girl's life, and she has done it with someone else. In the back of my head it feels like the wobbling glass of water in *Jurassic Park*, a warning of the time when she will escape my influence altogether.

But until then, I shall face the pink blizzard. Or at least keep my head up. I might even let her have the ballet lessons, on condition she keeps up the karate or, if she goes off that, boxing.

Or maybe I'll just buy her a gun. A pink one, of course.

25 0800: How's My Mothering?

The continual changes of behaviour – the children's, and therefore ours – are beginning to take their toll. The childcare books that were around when they were babies have given way to child-management manuals, with chatty titles like *How to Talk So Your Child Will Listen* and *Listen So Your Child Will Talk*. Some, like that one, actually do make some sense. But they tend to assume a progressive scenario, where the correct application of behaviour modifying strategies, and the increasing age of the children, combine to create an ever more harmonious domestic scene. What they don't describe is the sensation of going backwards, and how a civilized meal for four can descend in minutes into a trailer for *The Jerry Springer Show*.

In the horrible West Country pub, still arguing over Lydia's chips, or lack of them, I ponder how quickly we can change from civilized people – us talking, the children drawing – into monsters. And I think about how

tired I am of it all. Tired of Peter pretending to be so
bloody reasonable all the time. Tired of children whose
needs I'm supposed to put first. All the time! I'm not a
mother, I'm a servant. All that stuff they leave on the
floor. I am SICK SICK *SICK* of it! Even when I began
to actually want children, I never counted among my
ambitions '*to get a job as a slave*'. Hey, Gloria Steinem!
Remember when you couldn't understand why you felt
such solidarity with black women? Then you realized it
was because you all belonged to the Female Underclass.
I'm with you, baby! I'm *there*! Right now I am so identified
with those Filipina maids locked up by mad, rich employ-
ers who take their passports away – if you spoke to me
I'd answer in Tagalog. The kids roam the house, discard-
ing clothes, swords, wands, marbles, toast and Lego, and
I follow, almost permanently on my knees. Bending and
picking, bending and picking; I'm like an extra in *Gone
With The Wind*.

And at the same time, I feel this:

Somehow I've been allowed to become a parent, and
I still can't believe I've got away with it. Look, here I
am crossing the road with them. Here I am, driving
them down the motorway to my mother's. They are *in
my charge*. I can take them *anywhere*. I can take them *to
the park*. On *my own*. Really, is no one going to stop
me? It doesn't seem possible. I've got the Crown Jewels

here. *Me*. And I just *know* something bad's going to happen.

'Come *back*!'

'Get *down*!'

'That tree's way too high for you!'

'If you jump on there, you'll fall down and hurt yourself.'

'Don't climb up the outside of the stairs! You'll fall on the tiles and crack your head open!'

'Hold my hand when we cross the road! Don't pull away!'

'The drivers can't *see* you! Don't you realize?!!'

'If you run across that road without holding my hand you'll get hit by a car . . .'

I can't let go of their hands or they'll jump in front of a car. Lorries have magnets that will drag them under the wheels. I can't let them out of the swings enclosure because they'll run off and not come back. A centrifugal force will propel them away from me and they'll be gone forever, like the beads of a necklace spilled down a drain. I've got to anchor them somehow. I should be the centre of their orbit, but I have no gravitational pull. This is how you end up being over-protective. *This* is how you end up with them still living at home at forty-five in cardigans, watching every episode ever made of *Blake's Seven*. It's not cruelty: it's fear. I lie awake seeing terrible things: snuff movies that wait for the hours of deepest darkness and switch themselves on in my head.

In the park once, we saw a man with a baby in a pushchair. He was OK-looking but a bit wet, the sort of man we'll probably encourage Lydia to go out with on the grounds that he won't insist on sex. He was being *so* nice to this kid: 'Look at those ducks! They're swimming, aren't they? Oh! Would you like your hood pulled back a little bit? *That's* better!'

My two were whining for food. I offered them apples, which they didn't want, and then they saw the chocolate biscuits I was saving for later. I handed over the biscuits and growled at them for dropping the wrappers on the ground. Then I growled at them for getting chocolate on their fleeces. Then I growled at them to be quieter: there are other people trying to enjoy the ducks, you know! Next to this guy and his baby we were like those families you hope won't come near you on holiday, who just shout, consume and exist in their own ecosystem of crap. I was sure he'd decided I was called Britney and had a tattoo.

As they moved off towards the swings Lydia said, 'Why has that baby got that thing on its face?' It was a drip. The poor little thing had a tube in its nose, with a huge-looking piece of tape to hold it in place. It was ill. No wonder its dad was being so nice. My children were perfect and I was growling at them. If they'd had something wrong with them, perhaps I'd have been nice too. But since they weren't dying or anything I could afford to growl. And then I felt terrible.

While I've been thinking this, Peter has persuaded Lawrence to give up some of his chips in return for advance ownership of the chocolate that comes with the coffee. Lydia's not entirely happy with this arrangement, not surprisingly since there'll only be one chocolate because I'm not having coffee; I'm killing my husband and going back to London instead. Peter orders them ice creams, and finishes up with the Deluxe Special, the line that comes just before they shove you in the attic and turn the key.

'Look, why don't you go off and relax? I'll handle this.'

'Why don't you fuck off?'

I go out to the car and half read the paper. And it occurs to me that the period we're always looking ahead to, the Calm Time, when life stops being so volatile, is something we've just imagined. When they were babies we looked forward to their walking and talking, but that presented a new set of challenges, such as falling downstairs and answering back. When they were toddlers we looked forward to their feeding themselves, and learning to read, but that provoked new challenges such as eating ve-ry slow-ly and whining at us when we turned out the light. At each stage we've envisaged a plateau, a resting place where, after a steep climb, the landscape flattens and opens out. And I realize that like the person who thinks that getting married is the solution, rather than merely the opportunity to fight with the same person each day instead of different ones, we have fundamentally misunderstood the whole thing.

What we have to look forward to are just a variety of ever-changing scenarios which we are unable to control or predict. Round the corner we almost certainly have some form of best friend, she-loves-me-she-loves-me-not soap operas for Lydia, and being shoved by larger boys with stubble, on or off the pitch for Lawrence. Then there'll be voices breaking, and meticulously planned parties to which the cool people may not come. And after that, hushed phone calls, doors slamming – *'What's the matter?' 'NOTHING!'* – and me and Peter fighting over who drives across town to collect them at 2 a.m., to be followed by driving lessons at £245 an hour. And beyond that, I can see worry: worry about their going to Burma in their gap year and falling in love with a dissident and going to jail; worry about their staying here and lying on their beds smoking dope for the rest of their lives; worry about their settling down too young; worry about their not settling down at all; worry about their not fulfilling their dreams, not being happy, not being well or getting run over on a road somewhere because at thirty-two they still forget to look both ways and look again. Worry about how they will cope with life when we're gone. Now I'm worrying about dying early and leaving them orphaned. If I let my mind roam, I can think of at least ten ways I could die tomorrow, without even leaving the house.

There is no Calm Time and never will be. This is a truly terrifying thought. I close my paper and ponder the immensity of it. Behind the trees, the sun is dropping. Peter and the children are coming towards me, laughing. They have charmed two more chocolates out of the waitress. Peter bends down and kisses me through the window.

'Hello, darling!'

He gets them into their seats and they each take a book out of the pocket as we drive off.

'Aren't they beautiful?'

'Yeah . . .'

And I know there aren't two people in the whole world I would rather have my life wrecked by.

Epilogue

I'm on my way out one evening, and Lawrence calls out
from his position in front of the TV: 'Good luck, Mummy!
If you get in any trouble, you know our phone number.'